Five Fractured Fairy Tales
For the Classroom
with Readers Theater

Differentiated to Meet the Needs of
All Students

For Grades 4-9

© Two Pencils and a Book

ISBN: 979-8324134105

The Science of Reading, Executive Function, Phonics and Equity in Literacy For Older Struggling Readers

© Two Pencils and a Book. All rights reserved. No part of this publication can be reproduced or transmitted in any form or by anyone except for the classroom use of the person who purchased this book. Any other reproduction is strictly prohibited.

For additional permission or questions email twopencilsandabook@gmail.com

Table of Contents

Elements of Fairy Tale Interactive Notebook Pages — page 7
There is an option presentation in PDF and in Google Slides:
Elements of a Fairy Tale vs. Elements of Fractured Fairy Tales:
https://docs.google.com/presentation/d/1fDcGFyQIklUeNxHOZ1rAuAsMfsj_G7NiLRmtrGTI2kw/edit?usp=drive_link

<u>Jack, Cinderella and the Algebra Final</u> — page 11
    Story
    Story Version 2 at LL 450L – ATOS 3.22
    Readers Theater
    Comprehension Assessment
    Fluency LL 300L – ATOS 2.32
    Fluency LL 650L – ATOS 4.5
    Fluency LL 1100L – ATOS 8.0
    Constructed Response Question – Story Elements
    Theme, Setting, Character Traits, Main Idea, Problem, Solution Student Page
    Corresponding PowerPoint
    https://docs.google.com/presentation/d/1iKFYQVbV9N9UTY7gbpMwzl5cLXemz6IIMvrpNnBDv3w/edit?usp=sharing

    Interactive Notebook Pages
        Compare and Contrast
        Theme
        Character Traits
        Inference – Dialogue
        Inference Questions Specific to the Story
        Key Idea and Details
        Theme
        Sequence of Events
        Point of View
        Think Pair Share – Characters, Plot and Theme — page 40

<u>The Wicked Witch of Summer</u> — page 41
    Story
    Story Version 2 at LL 350L – ATOS 2.53
    Readers Theater — page 48
    Comprehension Assessment
    Constructed Response Questions – Inference, Theme, Character, Dialogue, Figurative Language
    Theme, Setting, Character Traits, Main Idea, Problem, Solution Student Page
        Interactive Notebook Pages
        Compare and Contrast
        Theme
        Character Traits
        Inference – Dialogue
        Inference Questions Specific to the Story
        Key Idea and Details
        Theme
        Sequence of Events
        Point of View
    Think Pair Share – Characters, Plot and Theme

<u>Summer Jobs, Captain Hook and a Dragon 1.0</u> — page 73
    Comprehension Assessment
    Summer Jobs, Captain Hook and a Dragon 2.0 – 410L-600L – ATOS 3.95
    Comprehension Assessment
    Readers Theater — page 83

Whole Class Activity – Compare and Contrast   page 85
    Theme, Setting, Character Traits, Main Idea, Problem, Solution
    Interactive Notebook Page
        Compare and Contrast
        Theme
        Character Traits
        Inference – Dialogue
        Inference Questions Specific to the Story
        Key Idea and Details
        Theme
        Sequence of Events
        Point of View
    Think Pair Share – Characters, Plot and Theme

The County Fair   page 103
    Reading Comprehension   page 107
The County Fair V.1 LL 410L-600L – ATOS 3.5
    Reading Comprehension
    Readers Theater
    Interactive Notebook Pages
        Key Ideas and Details RL.2 – Theme Development Interactive Notebook
        Story Events
        Plot Diagram – there is a PDF presentation as well as a Google Slides presentation at
        https://docs.google.com/presentation/d/1UdRNIrVVkpIwkdipBHQqVYffRtXhwv1veQSgWKwC7uU/edit?usp=sharing
        Plot Diagrams for Versions 1 and 1 of "The County Fair"   page 120
        Think Pair Share – "The County Fair   page 124

Expand the Story – Write a Narrative – "The County Fair Next Year"   page 125
Elements of a Fairy Tale Interactive Notebook Page   page 127
Analyze the Impact of the Author's Choice   page 128

Compare and Contrast Two Versions General Worksheet   page 130

The County Fair Figurative Language   page 131
    Figurative Language Worksheet – there is a corresponding PDF presentation as well as a Google Slide presentation – Figurative Language Language Presentation for worksheet page____
    https://docs.google.com/presentation/d/1QeDP34Bzplc0oRvkw2zcLaDkD9gYLBRb46K3I_EahXU/edit?usp=sharing
Compare and Contrast – Story vs. Readers Theater   page 137

Fluency Research and Script   page 138

Elements of a Fairy Tale vs. Elements of Fractured Fairy Tales:
https://docs.google.com/presentation/d/1fDcGFyQIklUeNxHOZ1rAuAsMfsj_G7NiLRmtrGTI2kw/edit?usp=drive_link

Elements of Fiction "Jack, Cinderella, and the Algebra Final" Presentation:
https://docs.google.com/presentation/d/1UL9HI1ZqD-2Go2n8n4ycxdD51dJCjn18oL3JXMrh7Co/edit?usp=sharing

The County Fair Plot Diagram:
https://docs.google.com/presentation/d/1UdRNIrVVkpIwkdipBHQqVYffRtXhwv1veQSgWKwC7uU/edit?usp=sharing

Figurative Language Language Presentation for worksheet page____
https://docs.google.com/presentation/d/1QeDP34Bzplc0oRvkw2zcLaDkD9gYLBRb46K3I_EahXU/edit?usp=sharing

Teacher Page

Teacher Notes and Optional Lesson Plan

Prep: Divide class into groups by Readers Theater Script
- Jack, Cinderella, and the Algebra Final (RT page 11) – 6 parts
- The Wicked Witch of Summer (RT page 43) – 9 parts
- Summer Jobs, Captain Hook and a Dragon (RT page 75) – 11 parts
- The County Fair (RT page 103) – 9 parts
- The County Fair Figurative Language

NOTE: I like to let my students work in teams or pairs. I let them talk but tell them the conversation needs to be about the stories. I walk around and ask story questions while they work.

I work through the unit over two weeks. I divide the class into groups and assign parts based on the scripts. The scripts are differentiated – some parts are big, and some contain fewer lines.

Lesson 1: Elements of Fractured Fairy Tale
- Elements of a Fairy Tale vs. Fractured Fairy Tale Google Slide Presentation: https://docs.google.com/presentation/d/1fDcGFyQIklUeNxHOZ1rAuAsMfsj_G7NiLRmtrGTI2kw/edit?usp=sharing with worksheet
- Then partner activity: "Choose Your Favorite Fairy Tale," fill out the interactive notebook graphic organizer on page 7
- **Discuss favorite fairy tales and how they can be twisted.**

Lesson 2: Read together, alone, in pairs or groups "Jack, Cinderella, and the Algebra Final." I usually do pairs.
- Do literature response activities
- Do Fluency – there are three levels of the summary for fluency practice differentiation
- DO GOOGLE SLIDE OR PDF – STORY ELEMENTS
- Do Comprehension
- Interactive Notebook pages (INP)
- HAVE THIS GROUP PERFORM "Jack, Cinderella, and the Algebra Final."
- Think Pair Share

Lesson 3: Read together, alone, in pairs or groups "The Wicked Witch of Summer." I usually do pairs.
- Do Literature Response
- Comprehension
- Do Interactive Notebook Pages
- HAVE THIS GROUP PERFORM "The Wicked Witch of Summer" Readers Theater
- Think Pair Share

Lesson 4: Read together, alone, in pairs or groups "Summer Jobs, Captain Hook and a Dragon."
- Do Comprehension
- Do Literature Response
- Do Interactive Notebook pages
- HAVE THIS GROUP PERFORM "Summer Jobs, Captain Hook and a Dragon."
- Think Pair Share

Lesson 5: Read together, alone, in pairs or groups "The County Fair."
- Do Comprehension
- DO PLOT DIAGRAM – THERE IS A PDF AND GOOGLE SLIDE PRESENTATION
- Do Literature Response
- Do Interactive Notebook pages
- HAVE THIS GROUP PERFORM "The County Fair."
- Think Pair Share

Lesson 6: Expand the Story – Students work together to write their own narrative that expands on "The County Fair" – "The County Fair Next Year."

Lesson 7: Read aloud "The County Fair Figurative Language."
- Assign Figurative Language Worksheet
- Review Worksheet together using PDF presentation or GOOGLE SLIDE PRESENTATION

Lesson 8: Have students do page 124 comparing and contrasting their fractured fairy tale narrative to its readers theater version.

Alternative Option: If I am working with a group of students with learning differences – we work through all of the stories together.

Name: _____ # _____

Directions: Glue into your notebook for reference.

Elements of a Fairy Tale

ELEMENTS

Magic: The use of supernatural powers to make things happen that wouldn't happen in the real world. Magic can be found in objects, people (like witches or wizards), or creatures in the story.

Good vs. Evil: A battle between the good characters, like heroes or heroines, and the evil ones, like villains or monsters. Usually, good wins over evil by the end of the story.

Moral or Lesson: A teaching or main idea that the story is trying to pass on to you, like the importance of honesty or bravery.

Enchanted Setting: The place where the story happens, often a magical land or kingdom that doesn't exist in the real world, like an enchanted forest or a castle in the clouds.

Royal Characters: Kings, queens, princes, and princesses are common in fairy tales, often involved in the adventure or needing to be saved.

Quest or Journey: A difficult challenge or adventure that the characters go on. This could be a quest to find a magical object or to save someone in danger.

Transformation: A change in form or nature of a character or object. This could be a frog turning into a prince, a beast into a man, or a pumpkin into a carriage.

Happy Ending: Most fairy tales end with a positive resolution where the characters live "happily ever after."

Curses and Spells: A type of magic where someone is given a punishment or condition that only a specific action or event can undo

Name: _____ # _____

Directions: Choose your favorite fairy tale and fill out the form with its elements. Cut along the solid lines, fold on the dotted lines. Glue under the middle to make flaps. Glue the heading in your notebook as well.

Elements of a Fairy Tale

Magic		Good vs. Evil
Moral		Enchanted Setting
Royal Characters	Glue Here	Quest or Journey
Happy Ending		Transformation
Curses or Spells		My Review of the Story

8

Jack, Cinderella and the Algebra Final

Name: _____ # _____

Jack, Cinderella and the Algebra Final

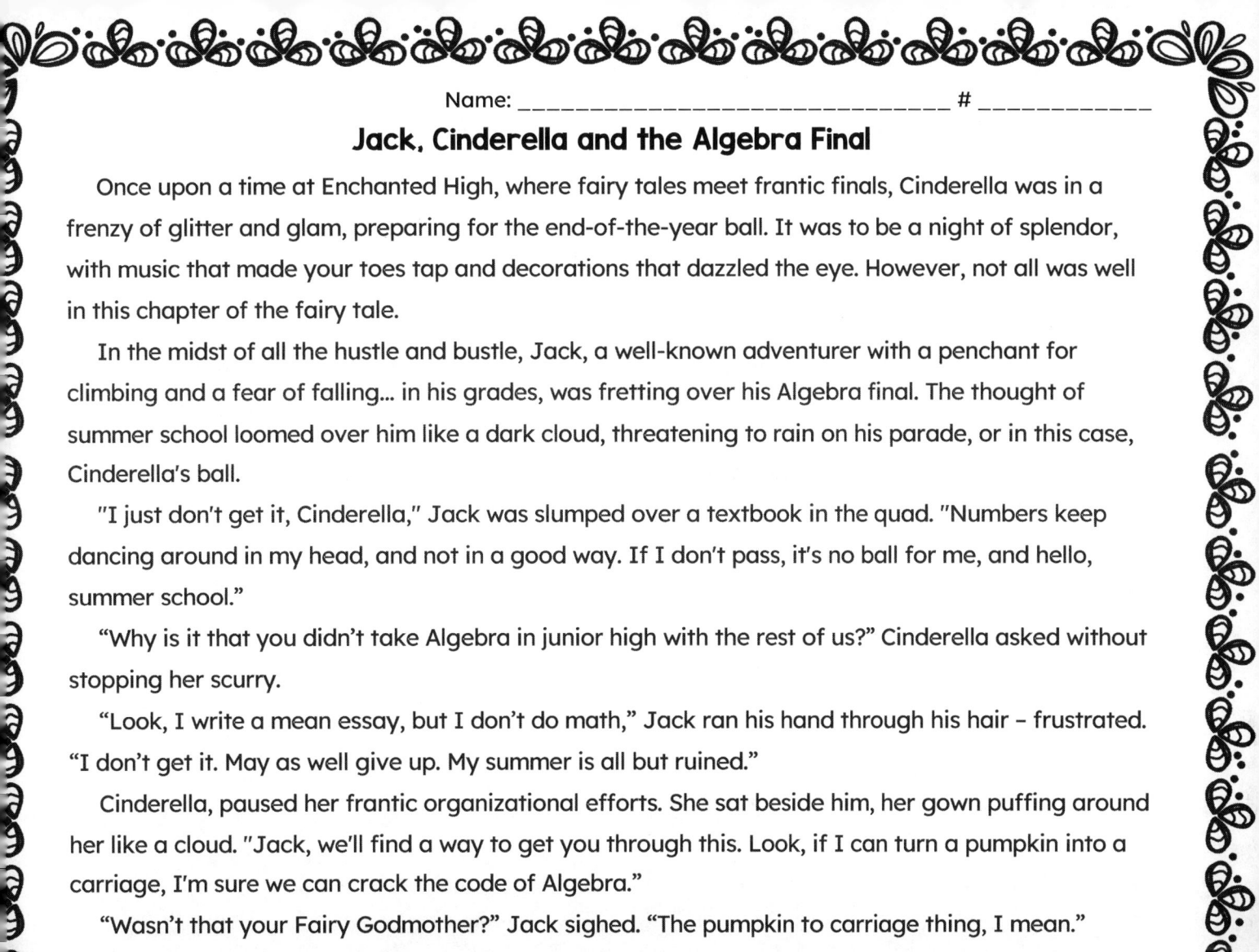

Once upon a time at Enchanted High, where fairy tales meet frantic finals, Cinderella was in a frenzy of glitter and glam, preparing for the end-of-the-year ball. It was to be a night of splendor, with music that made your toes tap and decorations that dazzled the eye. However, not all was well in this chapter of the fairy tale.

In the midst of all the hustle and bustle, Jack, a well-known adventurer with a penchant for climbing and a fear of falling... in his grades, was fretting over his Algebra final. The thought of summer school loomed over him like a dark cloud, threatening to rain on his parade, or in this case, Cinderella's ball.

"I just don't get it, Cinderella," Jack was slumped over a textbook in the quad. "Numbers keep dancing around in my head, and not in a good way. If I don't pass, it's no ball for me, and hello, summer school."

"Why is it that you didn't take Algebra in junior high with the rest of us?" Cinderella asked without stopping her scurry.

"Look, I write a mean essay, but I don't do math," Jack ran his hand through his hair – frustrated. "I don't get it. May as well give up. My summer is all but ruined."

Cinderella, paused her frantic organizational efforts. She sat beside him, her gown puffing around her like a cloud. "Jack, we'll find a way to get you through this. Look, if I can turn a pumpkin into a carriage, I'm sure we can crack the code of Algebra."

"Wasn't that your Fairy Godmother?" Jack sighed. "The pumpkin to carriage thing, I mean."

"Technicality, but I passed Algebra years ago," Cinderella said, but as the clock ticked closer to the ball – Jack still couldn't master the flash cards Cinderella helped him make.

By then, the tension was as thick as the fairy tale book on library's top shelf. In a stroke of inspiration, Cinderella summoned her Fairy Godmother, not for a dress or a coach, but for a tutoring session to remember.

"My dear, I specialize in transformations, not trigonometry," the Fairy Godmother chuckled, her wand at the ready.

"But you can transform my chances of passing, can't you?" Jack quipped, a hopeful glint in his eye.

Armed with nothing but a wand and wit, the Fairy Godmother did what she does best—she made magic happen. With a flick and a swish, she conjured up the most enchanting study guides, filled with tips and tricks, and potions for concentration. She even made magical mirror taught Jack to work the problems, then reflected the correct answers when Jack reasoned them out loud.

"This is all you've got?" Jack asked. "I was hoping for a Bibbidi-Bobbidi-Zappo-Bammo automatic A."

11

Jack, Cinderella and the Algebra Final - page 2

"Cheater's never win, my dear, and winners never cheat. Besides it's against union rules. Things have never been the same after the incident at Hogwarts."

"You don't want to cheat Jack. You can do it. You just need a little confidence," Cinderella smiled.

"Do you have any of that in your wand?" our beanstalk climbing friend pointed to the wand.

The Fairy Godmother lifted her wand and let loose – landing Jack on his tush by the reference section. "Think of what you do well when you study, and the answers will come."

The night before the exam, the library was alive with the sounds of flipping pages and whispered incantations. "Remember, Jack," Fairy Godmother advised, "the magic is not in the answers, but in understanding the questions."

The day of reckoning came. Jack faced his Algebra final with a bravery that rivaled his climb up the beanstalk. With every question, he imagined he was outsmarting giants again, only this time, the giants were algebraic expressions.

Meanwhile, Cinderella was putting the finishing touches on the ballroom. Her mind was equally split between hope for Jack and the perfection of the evening. As the final bell rang, signifying the end of the exam, a silence enveloped the school. It was as if the entire fairy tale world held its breath.

Then, out of the silence, came a cheer so loud it could wake Sleeping Beauty without a prince's kiss. Jack had done it; he had passed his Algebra final with flying colors.

The ball was everything one could hope for and more. The floors shone like glass, the music filled every nook and cranny with joy, and the laughter was contagious. Jack and Cinderella shared a dance, a moment of triumph over the trials of Algebra.

"Looks like you didn't need a magic bean to climb this beanstalk," Cinderella teased.

Jack laughed, spinning her around. "No, just a Fairy Godmother and a friend who believed in me."

As the night drew to a close, the Fairy Godmother approached, her eyes twinkling with pride. "It seems my work here is done. Remember, the real magic was in you all along."

And with a pop and a sparkle, she vanished, leaving behind a night of memories and a tale of friendship, magic, and a triumph over numbers. As for the Algebra, it was no longer an insurmountable giant but just another adventure conquered in the storybook of their lives.

And they all lived mathematically ever after. The end.

ATOS 3.22
LL @ L450

Name: _____ # _____

Jack, Cinderella and the Algebra Final - V2

Once upon a time at Enchanted High, Cinderella was busy getting ready for the big end-of-year ball. It was going to be a magical night. But not everything was going well. Jack was known for climbing up beanstalks. He was not known for his math skills. Now, he was worried about his Algebra final. If he didn't pass, he would have to go to summer school. And he would miss the ball.

"I just don't get Algebra," Jack told Cinderella. "I have to pass. If I don't, I'll have to go to summer school. I'll miss King Author's Knight Camp."

"I'll help you. Let's make flash cards. We can use some of these streamers," she said.

They made flash cards. And Jack studied. He studied hard. But he still didn't get it.

"I hate numbers," Jack said.

Cinderella didn't want Jack to miss the ball. And time was running out.

So, Cinderella called her Fairy Godmother (FG) for help. The FG didn't know at first. Then she used her magic to make special study guides and a mirror that Jack how to work the problems, but only after Jack tried solving the problems himself.

"Can't you just zap me up an A?" Jack asked.

"Cheaters never win. And winners never cheat." FG shook her head. "Besides I'm not allowed. Not after what happened at Hogwarts."

"You just need to believe in yourself," Cinderella said.

"Do you have any of that in your wand?" Jack asked the FG.

Jack wasn't sure this would work. He had hoped for an easy way to get an "A".

"We believed in you Jack." Cinderella said. "You got this."

"Just think of the answers like you do your adventures," the FG said. Then she zapped him with a spell of good will.

The night before the test, the library was full of magic and studying. The FG told Jack that understanding the problems was the real magic. The day of the test came. Jack was as brave as he was on his adventures. He pictured the questions as giants he had to outsmart.

Meanwhile, Cinderella was finishing the ballroom. She hoped Jack would pass. When he did, the whole school cheered. The ball was the best. It was a great kick-off for summer.

Jack and Cinderella celebrated his success together.

In the end, the Fairy Godmother reminded Jack that the real magic was in him all along. And after that, Jack saw Algebra not as a giant to fear but another adventure. They all lived "mathematically ever after".

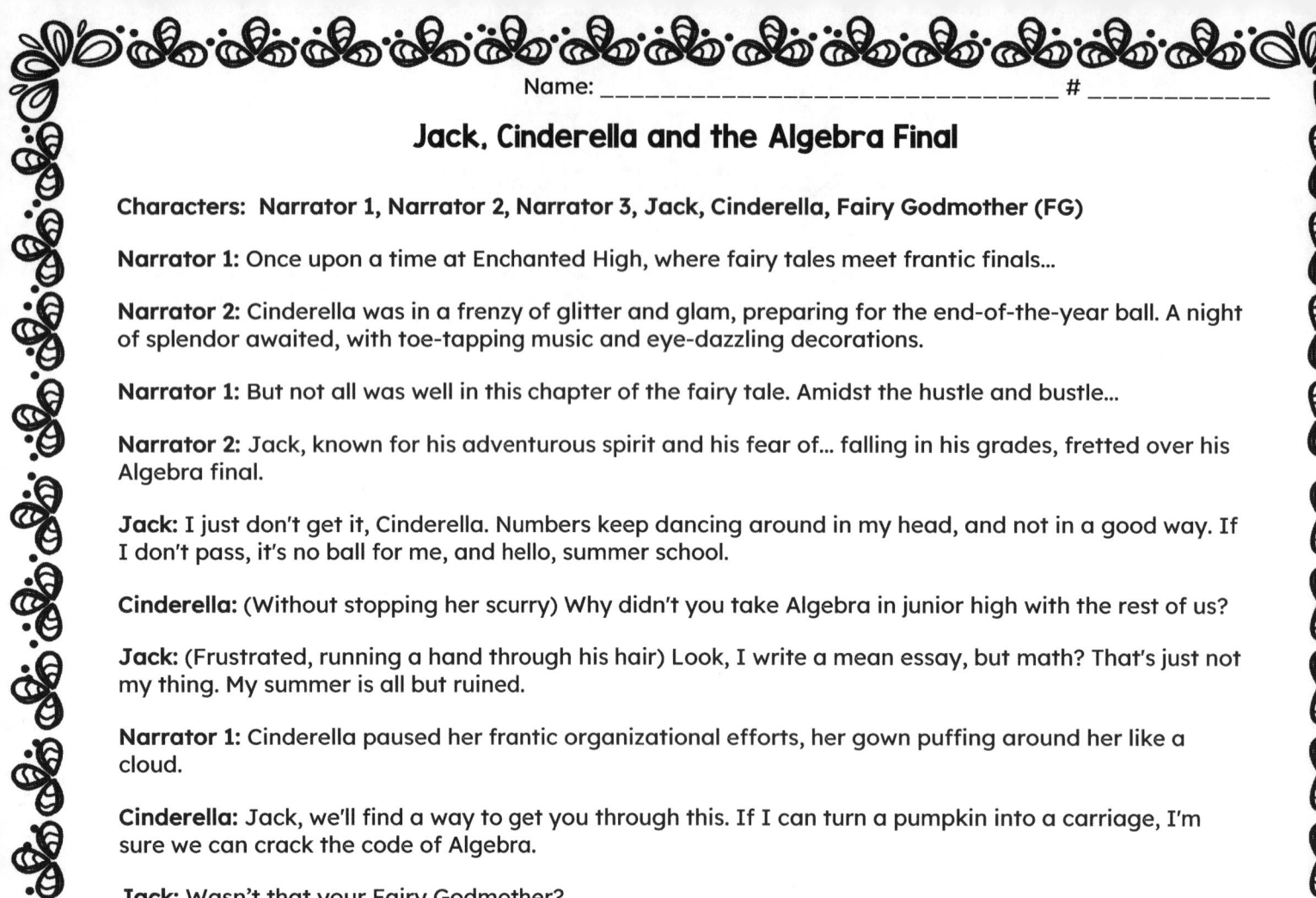

Name: _____ # _____

Jack, Cinderella and the Algebra Final

Characters: Narrator 1, Narrator 2, Narrator 3, Jack, Cinderella, Fairy Godmother (FG)

Narrator 1: Once upon a time at Enchanted High, where fairy tales meet frantic finals…

Narrator 2: Cinderella was in a frenzy of glitter and glam, preparing for the end-of-the-year ball. A night of splendor awaited, with toe-tapping music and eye-dazzling decorations.

Narrator 1: But not all was well in this chapter of the fairy tale. Amidst the hustle and bustle…

Narrator 2: Jack, known for his adventurous spirit and his fear of… falling in his grades, fretted over his Algebra final.

Jack: I just don't get it, Cinderella. Numbers keep dancing around in my head, and not in a good way. If I don't pass, it's no ball for me, and hello, summer school.

Cinderella: (Without stopping her scurry) Why didn't you take Algebra in junior high with the rest of us?

Jack: (Frustrated, running a hand through his hair) Look, I write a mean essay, but math? That's just not my thing. My summer is all but ruined.

Narrator 1: Cinderella paused her frantic organizational efforts, her gown puffing around her like a cloud.

Cinderella: Jack, we'll find a way to get you through this. If I can turn a pumpkin into a carriage, I'm sure we can crack the code of Algebra.

Jack: Wasn't that your Fairy Godmother?

Cinderella: Technicality, but I did pass algebra.

Narrator 3: The clock ticked closer to the ball – and the end of the year…

Narrator 2: But Jack still couldn't master the flash cards Cinderella helped him make. The tension was as thick as the fairy tale book on the library's top shelf.

Cinderella: It's time for some actual magic.

Narrator 1: And so, in a stroke of inspiration, Cinderella summoned her Fairy Godmother, not for a dress or a coach, but for a tutoring session to remember.

Fairy Godmother: My dear, I specialize in transformations, not trigonometry.

Jack: But you can transform my chances of passing, can't you?

Narrator 2: Armed with nothing but a wand and wit, the Fairy Godmother made magic happen.

Fairy Godmother: (With a flick and a swish) Behold, enchanting study guides and a magical mirror that reflects the correct answers, but only after you've tried to solve them yourself.

Jack: This is all you've got? I was hoping for a Bibbidi-Bobbidi-Zappo-Bammo automatic A.

Fairy Godmother: Cheaters never win, my dear, and winners never cheat, besides it's against union rules. Things have never been the same after the incident at Hogwarts.

Jack: I know those Gryffindors could not be trusted. Come on – just a little pixie dust or something.

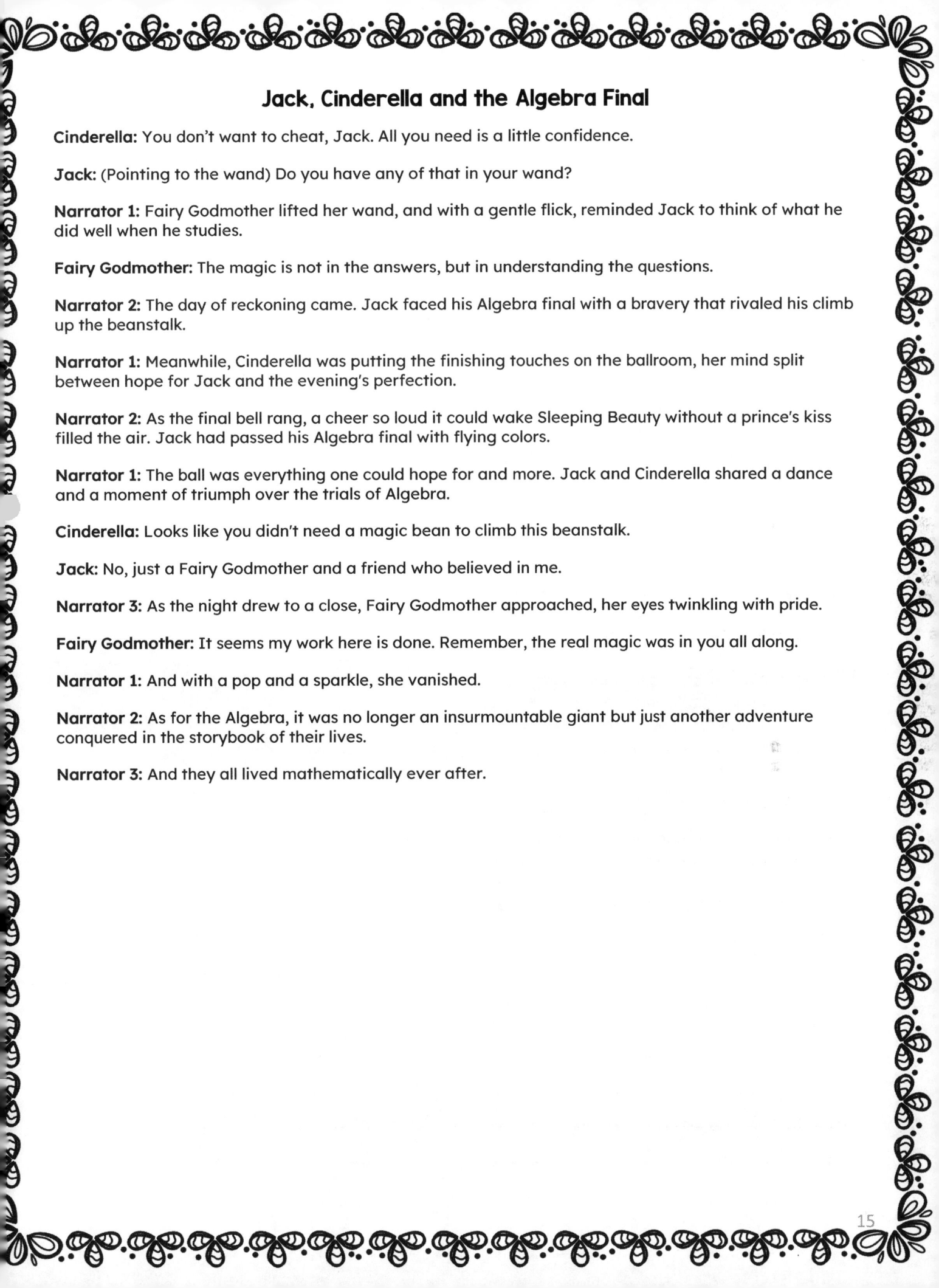

Jack, Cinderella and the Algebra Final

Cinderella: You don't want to cheat, Jack. All you need is a little confidence.

Jack: (Pointing to the wand) Do you have any of that in your wand?

Narrator 1: Fairy Godmother lifted her wand, and with a gentle flick, reminded Jack to think of what he did well when he studies.

Fairy Godmother: The magic is not in the answers, but in understanding the questions.

Narrator 2: The day of reckoning came. Jack faced his Algebra final with a bravery that rivaled his climb up the beanstalk.

Narrator 1: Meanwhile, Cinderella was putting the finishing touches on the ballroom, her mind split between hope for Jack and the evening's perfection.

Narrator 2: As the final bell rang, a cheer so loud it could wake Sleeping Beauty without a prince's kiss filled the air. Jack had passed his Algebra final with flying colors.

Narrator 1: The ball was everything one could hope for and more. Jack and Cinderella shared a dance and a moment of triumph over the trials of Algebra.

Cinderella: Looks like you didn't need a magic bean to climb this beanstalk.

Jack: No, just a Fairy Godmother and a friend who believed in me.

Narrator 3: As the night drew to a close, Fairy Godmother approached, her eyes twinkling with pride.

Fairy Godmother: It seems my work here is done. Remember, the real magic was in you all along.

Narrator 1: And with a pop and a sparkle, she vanished.

Narrator 2: As for the Algebra, it was no longer an insurmountable giant but just another adventure conquered in the storybook of their lives.

Narrator 3: And they all lived mathematically ever after.

Name: _____ # _____

Jack, Cinderella and the Algebra Final

1. Why was Jack worried about attending the end-of-the-year ball?
    a. He was struggling with his Algebra final.
    b. He was not invited by Cinderella.
    c. He had to finish a major essay.
    d. He didn't have the right outfit.

2. What was Jack's attitude towards Algebra?
    a. He found it easy but boring.
    b. He was confident and prepared.
    c. He was frustrated and ready to give up.
    d. He was indifferent and distracted.

3. How did Cinderella plan to help Jack with his Algebra?
    a. By transforming him into an Algebra genius.
    b. By making flashcards to help him study.
    c. By asking the Fairy Godmother to cast a spell on him.
    d. By hiring a professional tutor.

4. What was the Fairy Godmother's initial reaction to helping Jack with Algebra?
    a. She was confident and immediately started teaching.
    b. She was hesitant or didn't know if she should help at first.
    c. She refused to help, stating it was against her principles.
    d. She transformed Jack's textbooks into easier versions.

5. What magical aid did the Fairy Godmother provide for Jack's studying?
    a. A potion that would automatically give him the answers.
    b. Enchanting study guides and a magic mirror.
    c. A spell that made him understand all math concepts instantly.
    d. A time-turner to give him more time to study.

6. What was the outcome of Jack's Algebra final?
    a. He failed but was allowed to attend the ball anyway.
    b. He passed with the help of a spell during the exam.
    c. He passed using his own knowledge and the Fairy Godmother's aids.
    d. The exam was cancelled, and everyone passed automatically.

7. Summarize the story in six sentences.

_____
_____
_____
_____
_____
_____

Name: _____ # _____

Jack, Cinderella and the Algebra Final

1. Why was Jack worried about attending the end-of-the-year ball?
    <u>a. He was struggling with his Algebra final.</u>
    b. He was not invited by Cinderella.
    c. He had to finish a major essay.
    d. He didn't have the right outfit.

2. What was Jack's attitude towards Algebra?
    a. He found it easy but boring.
    b. He was confident and prepared.
    <u>c. He was frustrated and ready to give up.</u>
    d. He was indifferent and distracted.

3. How did Cinderella plan to help Jack with his Algebra?
    a. By transforming him into an Algebra genius.
    <u>b. By making flashcards to help him study.</u>
    c. By asking the Fairy Godmother to cast a spell on him.
    d. By hiring a professional tutor.

4. What was the Fairy Godmother's initial reaction to helping Jack with Algebra?
    a. She was confident and immediately started teaching.
    <u>b.</u> She was hesitant or didn't know if she should help at first.
    c. She refused to help, stating it was against her principles.
    d. She transformed Jack's textbooks into easier versions.

5. What magical aid did the Fairy Godmother provide for Jack's studying?
    a. A potion that would automatically give him the answers.
    <u>b. Enchanting study guides and a magic mirror.</u>
    c. A spell that made him understand all math concepts instantly.
    d. A time-turner to give him more time to study.

6. What was the outcome of Jack's Algebra final?
    a. He failed but was allowed to attend the ball anyway.
    b. He passed with the help of a spell during the exam.
    <u>c. He passed using his own knowledge and the Fairy Godmother's aids.</u>
    d. The exam was cancelled, and everyone passed automatically.

7. Summarize the story in six sentences.

At Enchanted High, amidst ball preparations, Jack struggles with Algebra, risking his ball attendance. Cinderella, despite her own preoccupations, promises support, eventually calling on her Fairy Godmother for magical tutoring. The Fairy Godmother's unconventional study aids, focusing on understanding and self-confidence, help Jack overcome his academic challenge. He passes his final, ensuring both can attend the celebratory ball, where their triumph over adversity is celebrated. The tale concludes with lessons on perseverance, the importance of support, and the power within, encapsulated by the phrase "lived mathematically ever after."

Jack, Cinderella and the Algebra Final

It's Enchanted High. A magical school for fairy tale kids. It's almost summer. For most of the school. All are excited for the big dance. It's the end of year party. Cinderella was planning it. But Jack was worried. Jack's not good at Algebra. He's not good at all. And he has a big final. If he fails it, there's no dance for him. And he'll have to go to summer school.

Cinderella tried to help Jack. She tried to help him with his math. It was hard. The dance was coming quickly. Summer was just a blink away. So, Cinderella asked her Fairy Godmother to help out.

The Fairy Godmother gave them magic study tools. She whipped up a magic mirror. He solved a problem. Reflected it in a mirror. It showed him correct answers. It showed him his mistakes.

The night before the test, they studied hard.

"Can't you just give me the answers?" Jack asked.

"You can't just know the answers. You have to understand the problems," Fairy Godmother said.

On test day, Jack felt ready. He looked at each question as a small challenge. Cinderella wanted the dance to be perfect. She hoped Jack would pass.

After the test, everyone cheered. Jack passed! No summer school!

The dance was fun. Cinderella and Jack partied!

"Thanks FG," Jack smiled. "I couldn't have done it without your magic."

"The real magic was in your hard work," she said. She flew off into the night.

And they all lived happily ever after.

Words Read: _____	Words Read: _____	Words Read: _____
minus mistakes: _____	minus mistakes: _____	minus mistakes: _____
equals wpms: _____	equals wpms: _____	equals wpms: _____

Jack, Cinderella and the Algebra Final

At Enchanted High, students were getting ready for an end of year dance. Cinderella was busy planning the event. But her friend Jack was worried. He was having a tough time with Algebra and feared failing. If he failed, he would miss the dance. He would also have to go to summer school.

Cinderella tried to help Jack with his math. They worked together, but Jack still found Algebra confusing. With the dance coming soon, Cinderella asked her Fairy Godmother for help. Instead of asking for a dress or a carriage, she asked for help with Jack's Algebra.

The Fairy Godmother used her magic. She created tools to help Jack learn. She made a magic mirror that explained the answers in a way Jack understood them. Then the mirror give him time to solve the problems. Last, it showed him the solutions.

The night before the test, they studied hard in the library.

"Can't you just give me the answers," Jack pleaded.

"The real magic is in understanding the questions," soothed Fairy Godmother.

On test day, Jack felt ready. He thought of each question as a challenge to beat. Cinderella was making sure the dance would be perfect. Everyone hoped Jack passed.

After the test, the school cheered. Jack passed! The dance was a big success. Cinderella and Jack celebrated.

"It was your hard work," Fairy Godmother told them. Then she disappeared.

The dance was the best! And summer vacation was even better.

Words Read: _____	Words Read: _____	Words Read: _____
minus mistakes: _____	minus mistakes: _____	minus mistakes: _____
equals wpms: _____	equals wpms: _____	equals wpms: _____

ATOS 8.0
1010L-1200L

Jack, Cinderella and the Algebra Final

At Enchanted High, where fairy tales and school tests come together, there was a lot | 15
of excitement about the upcoming end-of-the-year ball. Cinderella, a student at the | 30
school, was very busy getting ready for this magical night full of music, decorations and | 45
mad fun. But not everything was going smoothly. Jack, known for his love of adventure | 60
and climbing beanstalks, was having a hard time with his Algebra class. He was so | 75
worried about failing his final exam – which was highly likely. If he failed, it would be no | 92
dance for Jack. As for summer? It would be consumed with summer school. | 105

Cinderella, while preparing for the ball, took some time to try to help Jack with | 120
Algebra. However, despite making flash cards and studying hard, Jack still found the | 133
subject confusing. With the ball getting closer and Jack not making progress, Cinderella | 146
decided to ask her Fairy Godmother for help. | 154

The Fairy Godmother used her magic to create special study guides and a magical | 168
mirror that explained the problems in a way Jack understood them. This magical help | 183
was meant to encourage Jack to learn and understand Algebra, not just to give him the | 199
answers. | 200

The night before the exam, the library was filled with the sounds of pages turning | 215
and quiet voices as Jack studied with the magical tools he'd been given. The Fairy | 230
Godmother reminded him that understanding the questions was the real magic needed | 242
to succeed. | 244

When the day of the exam arrived, Jack felt as brave as he did when climbing giant | 261
beanstalks. He tackled each question with confidence, imagining them as challenges to | 273
be overcome. Meanwhile, Cinderella was making sure everything was perfect for the | 285
ball, hoping for Jack's success. | 290

After the exam, the school erupted in cheers; Jack had passed his Algebra final! The | 305
ball was a beautiful celebration of their hard work, filled with laughter and dancing. | 319

And everyone lived happily ever after. | 325

Words Read: _____	Words Read: _____	Words Read: _____
minus mistakes: _____	minus mistakes: _____	minus mistakes: _____
equals wpms: _____	equals wpms: _____	equals wpms: _____

Name: _____ # _____

Jack, Cinderella and the Algebra Final

1. Why do you think Cinderella insisted on helping Jack with his Algebra, despite being busy with the ball?

2. What is the central theme of the story and how is it shown through the characters and their actions?

3. How does Jack's attitude towards his Algebra final change throughout the story, and what events lead to this change?

4. How do the magical elements in the story contribute to its resolution?

5. How does the inclusion of the Fairy Godmother's magical tutoring session affect the plot and Jack's character development?

Teacher Page

Name: _____ # _____

Jack, Cinderella and the Algebra Final

1. Inference: Why do you think Cinderella insisted on helping Jack with his Algebra, despite being busy with preparations for the ball?

Cinderella's insistence on helping Jack with his Algebra, despite her busy schedule with the ball preparations, suggests her compassionate and caring nature. It indicates that she values friendship and the success of her friends over her own tasks and stresses. Cinderella's actions demonstrate her belief in the importance of support and teamwork, showing that she sees the well-being of her friends as a priority. This inference is supported by her determination to find a solution for Jack's academic struggle, reflecting her character as someone who goes above and beyond for those she cares about.

2. Theme: What is the central theme of the story and how is it conveyed through the characters and their actions?

The central theme of the story is the power of friendship, perseverance, and the belief in oneself to overcome challenges. This theme is vividly conveyed through the characters of Cinderella and Jack, as well as the Fairy Godmother. Cinderella and the Fairy Godmother's unwavering support for Jack illustrates the impact of friendship and belief in others. Jack's journey from despair to passing his Algebra final showcases perseverance and the importance of self-belief. Each character's actions and interactions highlight the idea that with the support of friends and confidence in oneself, any obstacle can be overcome.

3. Character Analysis: How does Jack's attitude towards his Algebra final change throughout the story, and what events lead to this change?

Jack's attitude towards his Algebra final transforms from defeat and resignation to hope and determination. Initially, he is overwhelmed by his inability to grasp mathematical concepts, which leads him to consider giving up. However, Cinderella's determination to help, her unwavering support, and the Fairy Godmother's magical intervention gradually instill confidence in him. The pivotal moment comes with the Fairy Godmother's enchanting study aids and her wisdom that the real magic lies in understanding, not in the answers themselves. These events collectively lead Jack to adopt a more positive outlook and approach his final with the bravery and cunning he used to outsmart giants, culminating in his success.

4. Textual Evidence: How do the magical elements in the story contribute to its resolution?

The magical elements, particularly the Fairy Godmother's intervention, play a crucial role in the story's resolution. Her ability to conjure enchanting study guides and a magical mirror that reflects the correct answers only after Jack attempts to solve the problems himself serves as a metaphor for discovering one's potential and the importance of effort. These elements do not solve Jack's problem directly but enable him to unlock his own ability to understand Algebra. This magical support underscores the story's message that while external help can provide guidance, true success comes from within oneself.

5. Analyzing the Conclusion: Reflect on the story's ending. How does the phrase "And they all lived mathematically ever after" tie back to the story's themes?

The phrase "And they all lived mathematically ever after" ties back to the story's themes by encapsulating the journey of overcoming academic challenges through friendship, perseverance, and belief in oneself. This whimsical twist on the classic fairy tale ending highlights the triumph over the specific challenge of Algebra, suggesting a future where the characters continue to apply the lessons learned from this experience. It reinforces the themes by implying that the skills of problem-solving, teamwork, and confidence gained will help them navigate future challenges, not just in mathematics but in life.

Name: _____ # _____

Jack, Cinderella and the Algebra Final

"Jack, Cinderella, and the Algebra Final," blends fairy tale elements with a modern school setting.

Theme: The primary theme revolves around the power of friendship, perseverance, and the belief that with the right support and a bit of magic (literal or metaphorical), any challenge can be overcome. It emphasizes that the real magic lies within oneself, not just in external aids.

Setting: The story is set at Enchanted High, a fantastical school where fairy tale characters navigate the challenges of modern teenage life. This setting combines elements of magic and contemporary schooling, including the pressure of finals and social events like balls.

Character Traits

- **Cinderella**: Resourceful and supportive, demonstrating her willingness to help a friend in need. She shows creativity in solving problems and believes in the power of hard work and magic.

- **Jack**: Adventurous but struggling academically, particularly with Algebra. He shows vulnerability in his fear of failure but ultimately displays courage and determination.

- **Fairy Godmother**: Wise and humorous, with a knack for magical solutions that require personal effort. She symbolizes the external support system that guides and facilitates personal growth.

Main Idea: The main idea is that challenges, whether academic or personal, can be overcome with the help of friends, determination, and a little bit of creative thinking. It underscores the importance of believing in oneself and the power of education and friendship.

Problem: Jack is at risk of failing his Algebra final, which would result in him having to attend summer school and miss the end-of-the-year ball. This academic struggle is the central conflict around which the story revolves.

Solution: With the combined efforts of Cinderella and the Fairy Godmother, Jack is provided with magical study aids that require his effort to work. This innovative approach to studying helps Jack pass his exam, demonstrating that success is a blend of support, hard work, and self-belief.

Overall, this story delivers a message of hope and resilience, wrapped in a delightful blend of fantasy and reality, encouraging readers to face their giants, whatever form they may take.

Name: _____ # _____

Jack, Cinderella and the Algebra Final
Compare and Contrast - Interactive Notebook

Directions: Cut along solid lines, attach at the dashed line. Make a book, one cloud on top the the other and attach to your notebook

What are the Similarities and Differences Between the Story and the Readers Theater?

Differences

Similarities

Name: _____ # _____

Jack, Cinderella and the Algebra Final Theme - Interactive Notebook

Directions: Cut along solid lines, attach at the dashed line. Make a book, one cloud on top the the other and attach to your notebook

The theme of
Jack, Cinderella and the Algebra Final

Teacher Page   Name: _____ # _____

Jack, Cinderella and the Algebra Final
Theme - Interactive Notebook

Directions: Cut along solid lines, attach at the dashed line. Make a book, one cloud on top the the other and attach to your notebook

The theme of
Jack, Cinderella and the Algebra Final

The theme centers on overcoming challenges through the power of friendship, perseverance, and self-belief. It portrays the journey of conquering academic obstacles with the support of friends and the realization that true strength lies within oneself.

Name: _____ # _____

Character Traits

Character traits are qualities or characteristics that describe what a person is like. It's how someone behaves and thinks.

Character Traits

Jack, Cinderella and the Algebra Final

Glue under here

Glue →

Actions: _____
_____
_____
_____

Thoughts: _____
_____
_____
_____

Defining Quote: _____
_____
_____
_____
_____

Cinderella

Actions_____
_____
_____
_____

Thoughts: _____
_____
_____
_____

Defining Quote: _____
_____
_____
_____
_____

Box 2

Jack

Directions: Cut along the outside of the shapes. Glue under the flaps. Glue Box 2 into your notebook. Glue Box one under flap on top and place on top of Box 2. Glue "Character Traits" under flap to create a cover for the pages on top.

27

Name: _____ # _____

Making Inferences RL.I   ## Jack, Cinderella and the Algebra Final

Directions: Cut along the outside of the shapes. Glue under the flap and attach it to your notebook to write under the flap. Choose a quote from the story. Write it under the "What Was Said" flap. Write what you think the quote means, or implies, under the "What It Implies" flap. What can you infer from your selected quote.

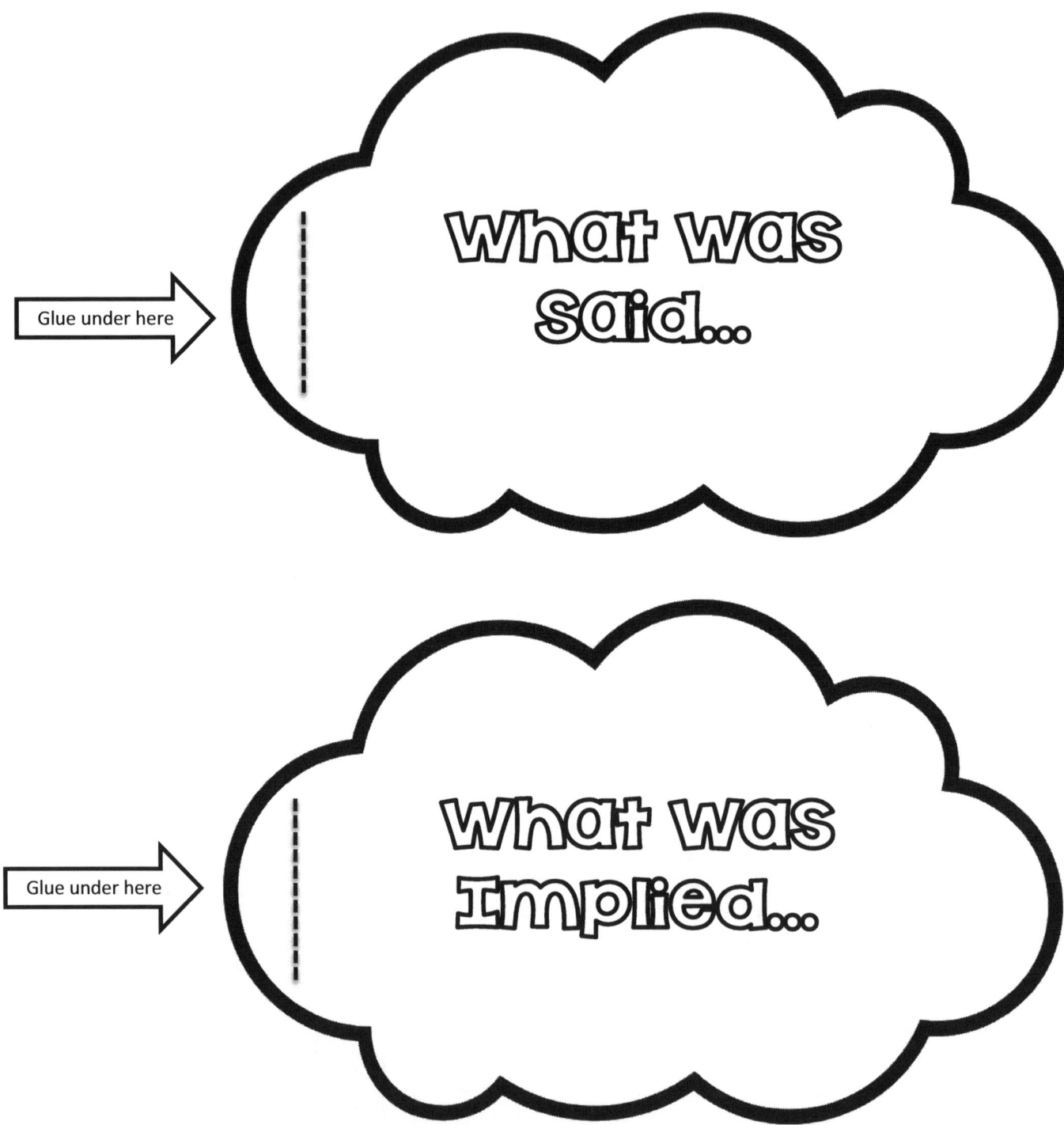

Inference: An inference is a conclusion drawn from evidence from your reading, your thoughts and what you know about life and events.

Name: _____ # _____

Making Inferences RL 1

Jack, Cinderella and the Algebra Final

Directions: Cut on the solid lines. Fold on the dotted lines. Glue or tape the center to your notebook. Answer the questions under the flaps.

Inference: An inference is a conclusion drawn from evidence in your reading, your thoughts and what you know about life and events.

Considering Cinderella's willingness to help Jack despite her busy schedule, what can we infer about her character and values?

Why do you think the author chose to set the story in a school where fairy tale characters attend? What can we infer about the message the author is trying to convey through this setting?

The Fairy Godmother refused to simply give Jack the answers, despite having the power to do so. What can we infer about her beliefs regarding education and personal growth?

Glue or tape here.

INFERENCE

29

Teacher Page   Name: _____ # _____

Making Inferences RL I

Directions: Cut on the solid lines. Fold on the dotted lines. Glue or tape the center to your notebook. Answer the questions under the flaps.

> **Inference:** An inference is a conclusion drawn from evidence from your reading, your thoughts and what you know about life and events.

Question 1: Why do you think the author chose to set the story in a school where fairy tale characters attend? What can we infer about the message the author is trying to convey through this setting?

Inferred Answer: The author likely chose this setting to blend the magical elements of fairy tales with the relatable experiences of school life, such as preparing for finals and attending school balls. We can infer that the author aims to convey that even in a world filled with magic, real-life challenges and personal growth are important themes. This setting allows the exploration of timeless values like friendship and perseverance in a context that young readers can relate to, suggesting that overcoming obstacles is a universal theme, regardless of the setting.

Question 2: Considering Cinderella's willingness to help Jack despite her busy schedule, what can we infer about her character and values?

Inferred Answer: Cinderella's actions suggest that she values friendship and empathy highly, placing Jack's needs alongside her own responsibilities. We can infer that she embodies qualities of selflessness and loyalty, demonstrating that helping others is a priority for her, even when she has her own tasks to manage. This implies a lesson that being there for others is an important aspect of friendship and character.

Question 3: The Fairy Godmother refused to simply give Jack the answers, despite having the power to do so. What can we infer about her beliefs regarding education and personal growth?

Inferred Answer: The Fairy Godmother's refusal to give Jack the answers directly, despite her magical abilities, suggests that she believes in the value of hard work and the learning process. We can infer that she views challenges as opportunities for growth, emphasizing the importance of earning one's success rather than taking shortcuts. This reflects a belief in the intrinsic value of learning and the idea that overcoming obstacles through one's effort is more rewarding and educational than easy victories.

Question 4: By the story's end, Jack has successfully passed his Algebra final, and the celebration at the ball is described in great detail. What can we infer about the significance of these events for Jack, Cinderella, and their peers?

Inferred Answer: The detailed description of the ball and Jack's success in passing his Algebra final signify more than just the end of the school year; they symbolize the culmination of hard work, friendship, and the overcoming of challenges. For Jack and Cinderella, these events mark significant personal achievements: Jack has conquered his academic difficulties, and Cinderella has played a key role in helping her friend succeed. For their peers, these events likely represent the joy of shared successes and the strength of their community. We can infer that these celebrations are a metaphor for the rewards of perseverance, the importance of support systems, and the value of education and friendship.

Name: _____ # _____

Key Ideas and Details RL.1: Cite textual evidence to support analysis of text, both inferential and explicit.

Directions: Cut along the outside of the shapes. Glue into your notebook. Glue under the flap and attach to write under the flap. Answer the question under the flap.

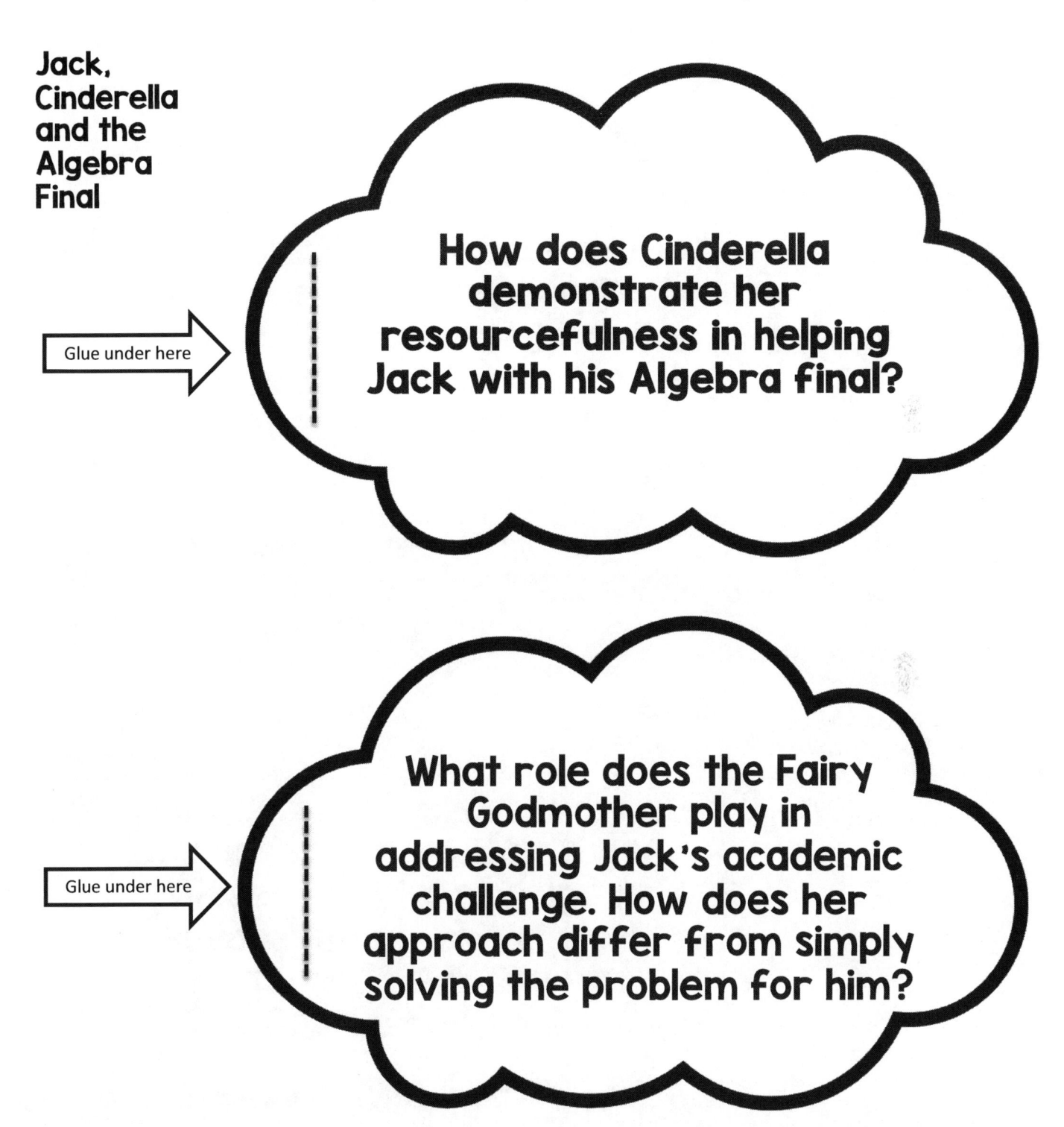

Jack, Cinderella and the Algebra Final

Glue under here →

How does Cinderella demonstrate her resourcefulness in helping Jack with his Algebra final?

Glue under here →

What role does the Fairy Godmother play in addressing Jack's academic challenge. How does her approach differ from simply solving the problem for him?

31

Name: _____ # _____

Key Ideas and Details RL.I: Cite textual evidence to support analysis of text, both inferential and explicit.

Directions: Cut along the outside of the shapes. Glue into your notebook. Glue under the flap and attach to write under the flap. Answer the question under the flap.

Jack, Cinderella and the Algebra Final

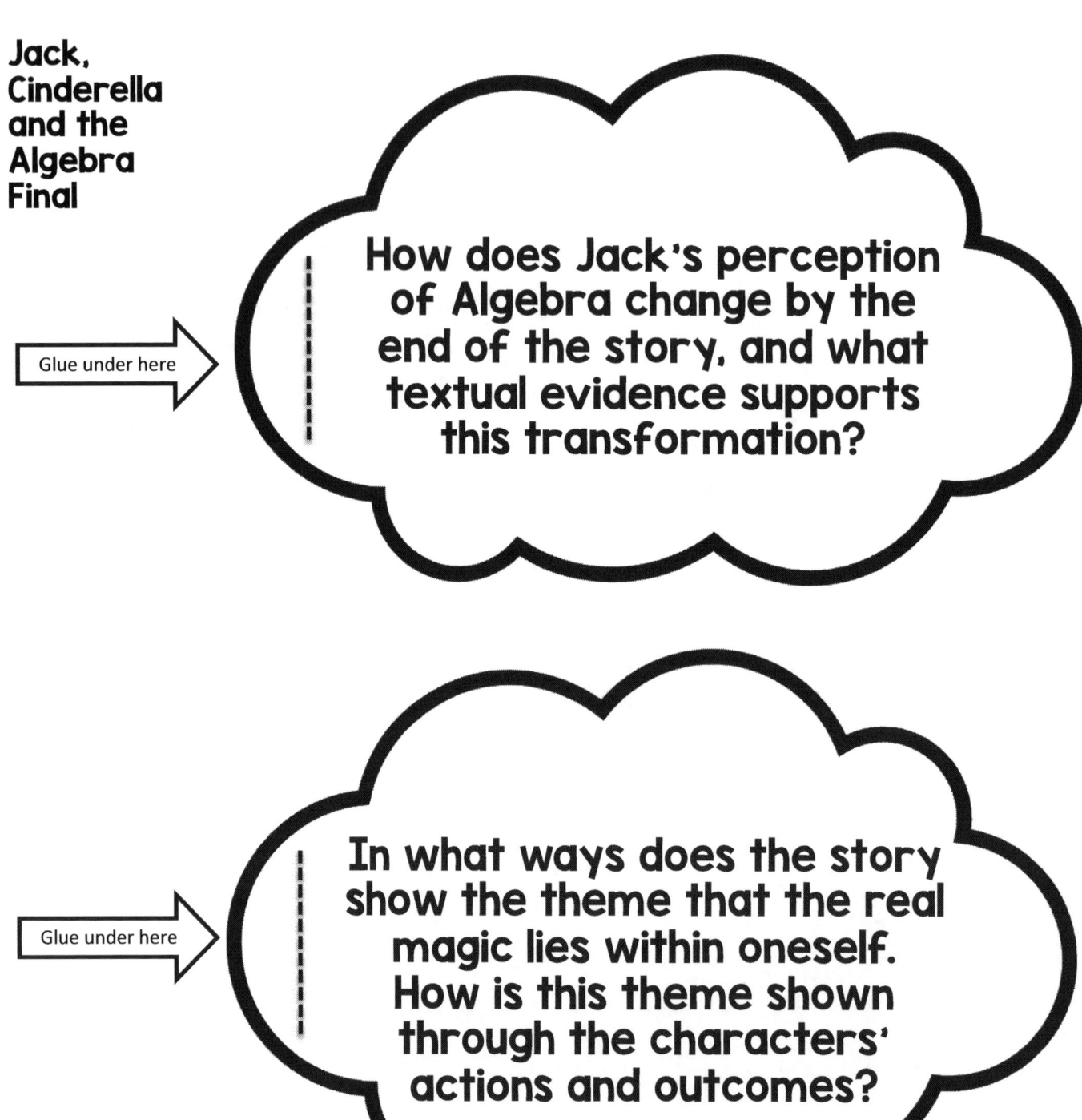

How does Jack's perception of Algebra change by the end of the story, and what textual evidence supports this transformation?

In what ways does the story show the theme that the real magic lies within oneself. How is this theme shown through the characters' actions and outcomes?

Teacher Page

Key Ideas and Details RL.I: Cite textual evidence to support analysis of text, both inferential and explicit.

Question 1: How does Cinderella demonstrate her resourcefulness in helping Jack with his Algebra final?

Answer Guidance: Students should identify specific actions taken by Cinderella that show her resourcefulness, such as making flashcards for Jack and summoning her Fairy Godmother for help. They should cite the moment when Cinderella decides to call upon her Fairy Godmother not for a dress or a coach, but for a unique tutoring session, demonstrating her ability to think creatively to solve problems.

Question 2: What role does the Fairy Godmother play in addressing Jack's academic challenge, and how does her approach differ from simply solving the problem for him?

Answer Guidance: Students should note that the Fairy Godmother provides magical study aids that require Jack's effort to activate, such as enchanting study guides and a magical mirror that reflects the correct answers only after Jack has attempted to solve the problems himself. This shows her role is not to give Jack the answers, but to facilitate his learning process, emphasizing the importance of personal effort. The text explicitly states, "Cheaters never win, my dear, and winners never cheat," highlighting her philosophy.

Question 3: How does Jack's perception of Algebra change by the end of the story, and what textual evidence supports this transformation?

Answer Guidance: Students should discuss how Jack's view of Algebra evolves from something overwhelming and insurmountable to a challenge he can overcome with determination and the right support. Evidence includes Jack facing his Algebra final "with a bravery that rivaled his climb up the beanstalk," and his success in passing the exam with "flying colors," which demonstrates his newfound confidence and understanding.

Question 4: In what ways does the story convey the theme that the real magic lies within oneself, and how is this theme exemplified through the characters' actions and outcomes?

Answer Guidance: Students should explore how the characters' actions, particularly those of Jack and Cinderella, embody the theme that true magic comes from within through perseverance, friendship, and self-belief. They should cite Cinderella's encouragement and belief in Jack, the Fairy Godmother's magical but effort-requiring aids, and Jack's ultimate success as evidence. The Fairy Godmother's parting words, "Remember, the real magic was in you all along," explicitly encapsulate this theme, underscoring the story's moral.

Name: _____ # _____

Key Ideas and Detail RL.2 - Theme Development

Jack, Cinderella and the Algebra Final

Theme <u>The Me</u>ssage. A theme is the moral or lesson of a story – it is the underlying meaning. **Analyze how the theme is developed throughout the story.**

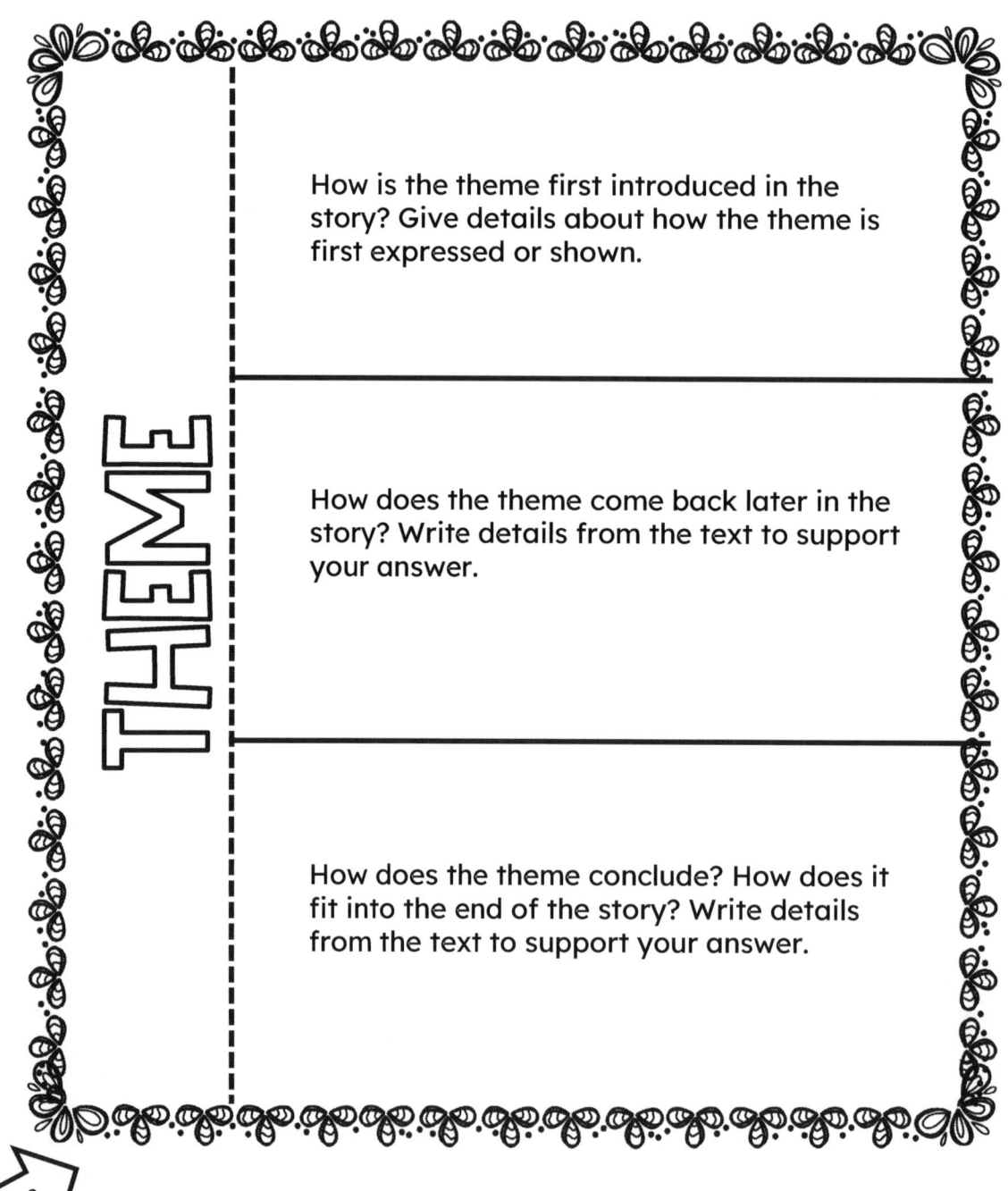

THEME

How is the theme first introduced in the story? Give details about how the theme is first expressed or shown.

How does the theme come back later in the story? Write details from the text to support your answer.

How does the theme conclude? How does it fit into the end of the story? Write details from the text to support your answer.

Glue under here

Directions: Cut along the solid lines. Fold along the dotted lines. Write your answer under the flaps.

34

Teacher Page   Name: _____ # _____

Key Ideas and Detail RL.2 - Theme Development

Jack, Cinderella and the Algebra Final

Theme <u>The Message</u>. A theme is the moral or lesson of a story – it is the underlying meaning.
Analyze how the theme is developed throughout the story.

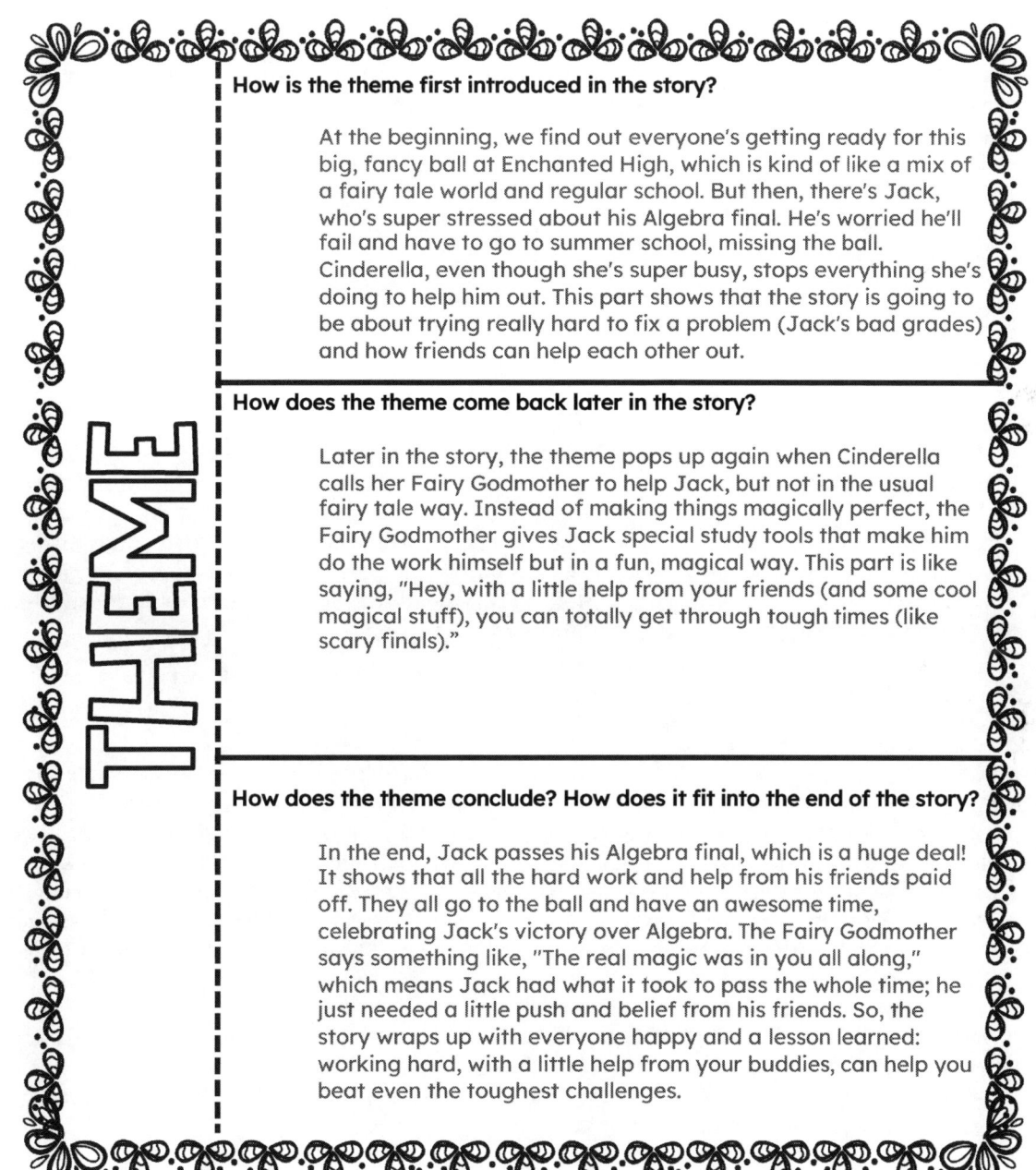

How is the theme first introduced in the story?

At the beginning, we find out everyone's getting ready for this big, fancy ball at Enchanted High, which is kind of like a mix of a fairy tale world and regular school. But then, there's Jack, who's super stressed about his Algebra final. He's worried he'll fail and have to go to summer school, missing the ball. Cinderella, even though she's super busy, stops everything she's doing to help him out. This part shows that the story is going to be about trying really hard to fix a problem (Jack's bad grades) and how friends can help each other out.

How does the theme come back later in the story?

Later in the story, the theme pops up again when Cinderella calls her Fairy Godmother to help Jack, but not in the usual fairy tale way. Instead of making things magically perfect, the Fairy Godmother gives Jack special study tools that make him do the work himself but in a fun, magical way. This part is like saying, "Hey, with a little help from your friends (and some cool magical stuff), you can totally get through tough times (like scary finals)."

How does the theme conclude? How does it fit into the end of the story?

In the end, Jack passes his Algebra final, which is a huge deal! It shows that all the hard work and help from his friends paid off. They all go to the ball and have an awesome time, celebrating Jack's victory over Algebra. The Fairy Godmother says something like, "The real magic was in you all along," which means Jack had what it took to pass the whole time; he just needed a little push and belief from his friends. So, the story wraps up with everyone happy and a lesson learned: working hard, with a little help from your buddies, can help you beat even the toughest challenges.

<u>Directions</u>: Cut along the solid lines. Fold along the dotted lines. Write your answer under the flaps.

Teacher Page

Key Ideas and Detail RL.2 - Theme Development

Jack, Cinderella and the Algebra Final

The central theme of overcoming challenges through perseverance, friendship, and a bit of ingenuity is subtly introduced and then fully developed throughout the story. Here's how the theme is presented, revisited, and concluded:

Introduction of the Theme

The theme is first introduced through the characters' preparation for the end-of-the-year ball at Enchanted High, juxtaposed with Jack's struggle with his Algebra final. While the setting is magical, the problems they face are incredibly relatable. Cinderella's willingness to help Jack despite her own busy schedule—preparing for a significant social event—lays the foundation for the theme. This moment shows that even in a world filled with magic, real-life problems like academic challenges still exist and that friendship and determination are vital in overcoming them. The line, "Cinderella, paused her frantic organizational efforts. She sat beside him, her gown puffing around her like a cloud," directly demonstrates Cinderella's commitment to helping a friend in need, emphasizing the importance of support and perseverance from the story's outset.

Development of the Theme

The theme is further developed when Cinderella enlists the help of her Fairy Godmother, not for her own benefit but to aid Jack in understanding Algebra. This act of seeking help and using resources creatively reinforces the theme of overcoming obstacles through perseverance and the support of friends. The Fairy Godmother's approach, providing enchanted study aids that require Jack's effort to be effective, underscores the message that success comes from one's own efforts augmented by support from others. This development phase is crucial as it illustrates the practical application of the theme: "Armed with nothing but a wand and wit, the Fairy Godmother did what she does best—she made magic happen," highlighting the blend of magic with personal effort.

Conclusion of the Theme

The theme culminates at the end of the story with Jack passing his Algebra final, enabling him to attend the ball. This outcome is not just a personal victory for Jack but a shared success celebrated by all characters involved. Cinderella's and the Fairy Godmother's efforts to assist Jack, coupled with Jack's newfound confidence and determination, reflect the story's moral. The celebration at the ball, described with vibrant detail, symbolizes the joy of overcoming obstacles through hard work, friendship, and a little bit of magic. The Fairy Godmother's parting words, "Remember, the real magic was in you all along," encapsulate the conclusion of the theme, emphasizing that the inner strength and determination of individuals, supported by their friends, are the true keys to overcoming life's challenges.

The story's end, "And they all lived mathematically ever after," ties the theme back into the narrative seamlessly, indicating that the lessons learned from overcoming this particular challenge will serve the characters well in future endeavors. It shows that the theme of overcoming challenges through perseverance, friendship, and ingenuity is not only central to this story but is a timeless lesson applicable in various contexts.

Through this progression, the theme is introduced, developed, and concluded in a way that is both engaging and educational, demonstrating the power of collective effort and internal resilience in the face of adversity.

Name: _____ # _____

Key Ideas and Detail RL.2 - Sequence of Events

Directions: Cut along the solid lines. Fold along the dotted lines. Write your answer under the flaps.

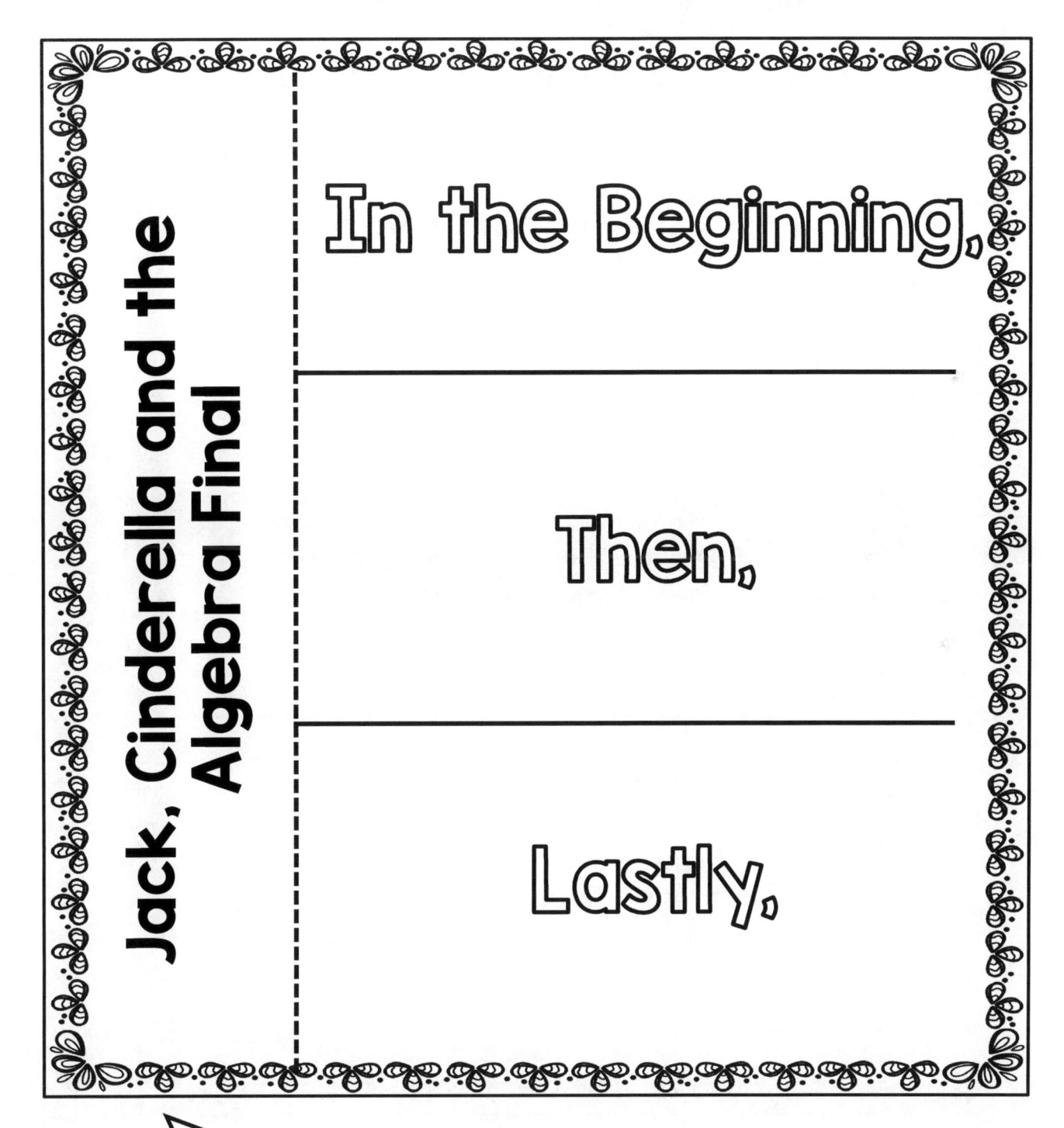

Jack, Cinderella and the Algebra Final

Jack, Cinderella and the Algebra Final

In the Beginning,

Then,

Lastly,

Glue Under Here

37

Name: _____ # _____

Key Ideas and Detail RL.6 - Point of View
Analyzing the Author's Attitude

Directions: Cut along the solid lines. Fold along the dotted lines. Write your answer under the flaps.

Analyze how the writer's attitude influences the beliefs of the characters.

Jack, Cinderella and the Algebra Final

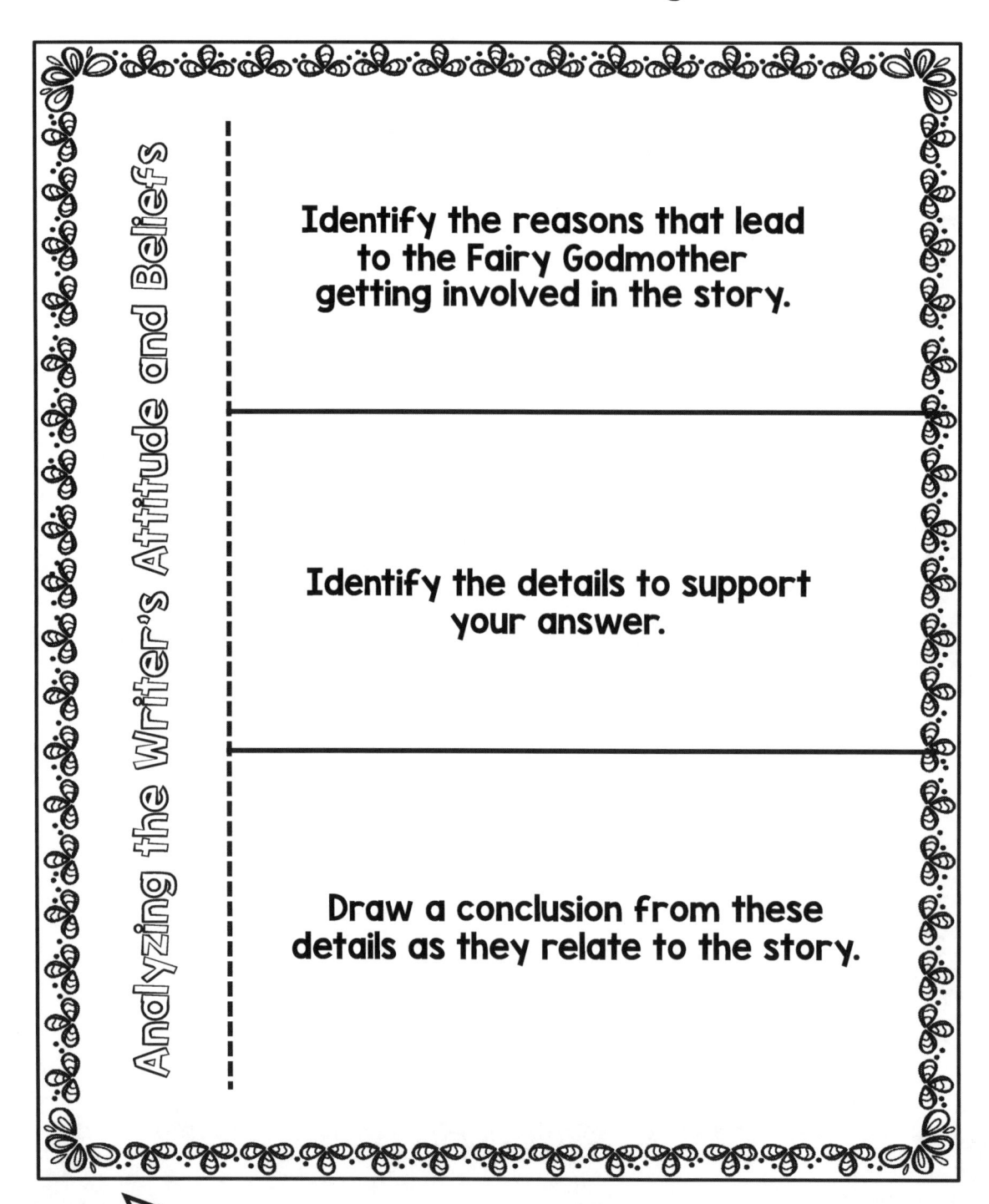

Analyzing the Writer's Attitude and Beliefs

Identify the reasons that lead to the Fairy Godmother getting involved in the story.

Identify the details to support your answer.

Draw a conclusion from these details as they relate to the story.

Glue Under Here

Teacher Page   Name: _____ # _____

Key Ideas and Detail RL.6 - Point of View
Analyzing the Author's Attitude

Directions: Cut along the solid lines. Fold along the dotted lines. Write your answer under the flaps.

Analyze how the writer's attitude influences the beliefs of the characters.

Jack, Cinderella and the Algebra Final

Analyzing the Writer's Attitude and Beliefs

Reasons the Fairy Godmother Got Involved

The Fairy Godmother got involved in the story because Cinderella was trying to help Jack pass his Algebra final, and they were running out of time and options. Cinderella had already tried to help Jack with flashcards, but it wasn't working, and the big end-of-the-year ball was getting closer. Jack was really stressed about the exam and was afraid he'd fail and have to go to summer school, which meant missing the ball. So, Cinderella thought of calling her Fairy Godmother for help, but not for a dress or a coach this time. She thought maybe her Fairy Godmother could do something magical to help Jack understand Algebra.

Details Supporting the Answer

1. **Cinderella's Initial Efforts:** The text mentions that Cinderella was helping Jack with flashcards, showing she was already trying to help him study.

2. **Jack's Struggle:** Jack tells Cinderella that numbers keep dancing around in his head in a bad way, indicating his frustration and fear of failing.

3. **Summoning the Fairy Godmother:** Cinderella decides to summon her Fairy Godmother as a last resort, hoping for a magical solution to Jack's academic problem.

Conclusion

From these details, we can conclude that Cinderella's determination to help her friend, combined with Jack's evident struggle and the urgency of the situation (with the ball approaching and the threat of summer school), are what led to the Fairy Godmother's involvement. This action highlights a key message of the story: friendship and creative thinking can lead to unique solutions in difficult times. The Fairy Godmother's involvement also underscores the theme that sometimes, external support is needed to overcome challenges, but it's the effort and determination from within that ultimately lead to success. Essentially, the story teaches that it's okay to ask for help and that together, we can find a way to solve even the toughest problems.

Name: _____   Partner: _____

Jack, Cinderella and the Algebra Final
Think - Pair - Share

Read "Jack, Cinderella, and the Algebra Final."

Part 1: Think (Individual Work) – Answer the questions.

Characters: List the main characters and their traits. _____
_____
_____

Plot: Summarize the key events in the story. _____
_____
_____
_____

Themes: Identify the themes or moral lessons in the story. _____
_____
_____
_____

Part 2: Pair (Discussion with a Partner)
Questions for Discussion:
- What makes the characters unique?
- How do they solve the crisis?
- How does the setting contribute to the story?
- What are some real-life lessons that can be learned from this story?

Problem-Solving: Brainstorm ideas on how you could change or add to the story to make it more interesting.
_____
_____
_____
_____
_____
_____

Part 3: Be Prepared to Share Out

One new idea you heard during the discussion: _____
_____
_____
_____

One point you agreed/disagreed with and why: _____
_____
_____
_____

The Wicked Witch of Summer

Name: _____ # _____

The Wicked Witch of Summer

In the heart of the Enchanted Forest, where trees whisper secrets and rivers sing symphonies, there was an air of unrest. Summer had dawned, but the sun's warm embrace was nowhere to be felt. The Wicked Witch of the West, known for her frosty heart and chilly demeanor, had cast a spell to cancel summer vacation, condemning the forest to an eternal state of spring cleaning.

"Why would anyone need more than one season? Spring has everything, clean air, rain, and endless chores!" cackled the Witch, stirring her cauldron with a broomstick that, frankly, had seen better days.

In a cozy cottage not too far away, Red Riding Hood, the Big Bad Wolf (who wasn't so bad once you got to know him, preferring the name BBG for 'Big Benevolent Gentleman'), Belle, the Beast (who was more of a softie than his name suggested), and Ana (of Arendelle fame), gathered around a flickering fire. They were all dreaming of Camp Evergreen, the summer camp they had been looking forward to all year.

"This is unbearable," Red huffed, her cape draped dramatically over the chair. "I had plans to master archery!"

"And I wanted to teach everyone the true art of howling at the moon. It's very misunderstood and not as easy as it looks," BBG added, his voice a deep rumble that vibrated the teacups.

Belle, ever the optimist, chimed in, "We can't let the Witch ruin our summer. There has to be a way to break the spell!"

The Beast, flexing his claws thoughtfully, suggested, "What if we invite her to camp? She's probably just lonely and...frosty."

Ana, with a spark of mischief in her eyes, proposed, "Or we could bring summer to her! Show her what she's missing! I live in a state of perpetual winter. I need my time at camp. I need to row, to hike, to swim...have any of you ever tried to swim in Arendelle?"

"We need a plan," Red said. "A real plan."

Just then, Jack bounced in from his latest beanstalk escapade. "Why so glum chums? And what's with the calendar? Mine's been stuck on Spring for weeks. I'm ready for those endless summer nights."

"It's the Wicked Witch of the West. She's cast a spell to stop summer," Ana said.

"But we've got a plan. Or we're coming up with a plan," Red said.

"We're thinking about inviting her to camp. Maybe she'll get in the summer spirit," Belle said.

"Look, I've whipped up an invite," the BBG opened an ornate pop-up card he made on the fly.

Name: _____ # _____

The Wicked Witch of Summer - page 2

"Did you just do that?" the Beast asked.

"That's amazing!" said Red.

"Just a little something I picked up from Grandma. She a whiz even without a Cricket," the BBG smiled.

"Who's going to bring it to her?" Ana asked.

"Not me," Jack said. "Ever since the golden goose incident – I'm not her favorite in the forest."

"Why don't you bring it to her Belle? You're least likely to be turned into a frog," the Beast said.

"Bring her these too," Ana said. "Give her no excuse not to come."

Armed with summer essentials—sunscreen, insect repellent, and an endless playlist of summer jams—the crew set off. BBG carried a portable beach, complete with sand and a collapsible palm tree. Red had a basket filled with summer reads and spectacular sun hats, while Ana concocted a magical summer breeze that followed them wherever they went. Belle led the way with the BBW's invitation in hand.

Upon reaching the Witch's castle, they were met with a blizzard. "Summer's over!" the Witch screeched, emerging from her icy fortress.

"Nice ice storm," Ana said. "They aren't easy to conjure."

The Witch eyed the princess from Arendelle. "Did you just say something nice to me?"

Jack nudged Belle. Belle stumbled forward. She held out the invitation.

"We wanted to give this to you," Belle said. "It's an invitation to summer camp."

"Summer camp? Me? What's the catch?" the Witch eyed the group before her. "Why are you being so nice? No one is ever nice to me. Anytime someone is - I look for falling houses."

"Wrong story," the Beast said. "What do you say? Don't you just love the summer?"

The Witch walked closer. "I never used to, but it may be growing on me. What's that smell?"

"Coppertone on a fresh summer breeze," Belle smiled.

"Will there be s'mores?" the Witch wavered.

"And popcorn balls and sailing and swimming and crafts and hiking and so, so much more. The whole deal. What'd you say?" Jack said.

"You!" the Witch pointed. "You stole that goose that got loose and caused the storm that brought the girl who dropped a house on me!"

"Bygones," the Beast pulled Jack to the back of the group. "Double chocolate s'mores and I'll even let you use my kayak," he coaxed.

Name: _____ # _____

The Wicked Witch of Summer - page 3

    The BBG stepped up and plopped his beach front and center. It instantly melted a circle in the snow, revealing green grass beneath. Belle's summer reads sparked curiosity in the Witch's eyes, and Ana's breeze softened the air around them.

    Finally, the Beast, with a shy smile, offered a sun hat to the Witch. "Summer is about warmth, not just in the air, but in our hearts," he said, his voice gentle. "We're offering camp and friendship."

    "And lots of s'mores," Red said.

    The Witch, who had never worn a sun hat or felt a warm breeze, found herself chuckling, genuinely, for the first time in centuries. "Well, I suppose one summer won't hurt. But only if I can join your camp as the official summer spell instructor! I want to contribute too."

    And so, summer vacation was saved, and Camp Evergreen had its most magical season yet, with the Wicked Witch of the West as the unexpected star. And s'mores were had by all.

Version 2 - 2.53
LL 350

Name: _____ # _____

The Wicked Witch of Summer

It's the heart of the Enchanted Forest. The trees whisper in the wind. The rivers sing. It's almost summer. But there was an air of unrest. It was almost summer, but it was still cold. Why? The Wicked Witch of the West – or WWW as she was called. She had a cold heart and a colder personality. She cast a spell to cancel summer vacation.

"Why do we need summer? Spring cleaning for all! We don't need more than one season. Spring has everything. It has clean air. It has rain. Best of all – it has endless chores!" cackled the Witch. She was stirring her pot with a broomstick. The broomstick, frankly, had seen better days.

Nearby Red Riding Hood, the Big Bad Wolf (who wasn't so bad once you got to know him, preferring the name BBG for 'Big Benevolent Gentleman'), Belle, the Beast (who was more of a softie than his name suggested), and Ana, sat by a flickering fire. They were all dreaming of Camp Evergreen. Camp Evergreen was the summer camp they went to. They'd been looking forward to all year.

"This is awful," Red huffed. "I had plans to master archery!"

"And I wanted to teach everyone how to howl at the moon. It's very misunderstood and not as easy as it looks," BBG added. He let out a loud howl.

Belle always looked on the bright side. "We can't let the Witch ruin our summer. There has to be a way to break her spell."

The Beast looked at his claws. Then he sat on them. "What if we invite her to camp? She's probably just lonely and...frosty."

Ana got excited. "Let's bring summer to her! Show her what she's missing! I live where it's always winter. I need my time at camp. I need to row. I need to hike. I need to swim. Have any of you ever tried to swim in Arendelle?"

"We need a plan," Red said. "A real plan."

Just then, Jack came down from his latest beanstalk escapade. "Why so glum chums? And what's with the calendar? Mine's been stuck on Spring for weeks. I'm ready for those endless summer nights."

"It's the the big WWW. She's cast a spell to stop summer," Ana said.

"But we've got a plan. Or we're coming up with a plan," Red said.

"We're thinking about inviting her to camp. Maybe she'll get in the summer spirit," Belle said.

"Look, I made an invite." The BBG opened pop-up card he made on the fly.

"Did you just do that?" the Beast asked.

"That's amazing!" said Red.

"Just a little something I picked up from Grandma." the BBG smiled.

"Who's going to bring it to her?" Ana asked.

"Not me," Jack said. "Ever since the golden goose. I'm not her favorite."

Name: _____ # _____

The Wicked Witch of Summer - page 2

"Why don't you bring it to her Belle? She won't turn you into a frog," the Beast said. "Probably."

"Bring her these too," Ana said. "Make her want to come."

They packed a basket. It was for the WWW. It had sunscreen. It had summer music. It had sand. It It even had a palm tree. Red had a basket filled with summer books. She also had hats. She had great sun hats. Ana brought up a magical summer breeze. It followed them wherever they went. Belle led the way with the BBG's invitation in hand.

They got to the Witch's castle. They were met with a blizzard. "Summer's over!" the Witch said. "Nice ice storm," Ana said. "They're hard to do."

The Witch eyed Ana. "Did you just say something nice to me?"

Jack pushed at Belle. Belle stumbled forward. She held out the invitation.

"We wanted to give this to you," Belle said. "Come to summer camp with us."

"Summer camp? Me? What's the catch?" the Witch asked. "Why are you being so nice? No one is ever nice to me. Anytime someone is – I look for falling houses."

"Wrong story," the Beast said. "What do you say? Don't you just love the summer?"

The Witch walked closer. "I never used to. But it may be growing on me. What's that smell?"

"Coppertone on a fresh summer breeze," Belle smiled.

"Will there be s'mores?" the Witch asked.

"And popcorn balls. There'll be sailing and swimming. There'll be crafts and hiking and so, so much more. What'd you say?" Jack said.

"You!" the Witch pointed. "You stole that goose. It got loose. It caused the storm. The storm brought the girl. The girl dropped a house on me!"

"Long time ago." The Beast pulled Jack to the back of the group. "Double chocolate s'mores. I'll even let you use my boat," he said.

The BBG stepped up. He plopped his sand and tree on the snow. It melted a circle in the snow, showing green grass beneath. Belle's books got the Witch's attention. And Ana's breeze softened the air around them.

Finally, the Beast, with a shy smile, offered a sun hat to the Witch. "Summer is about warmth, not just in the air, but in our hearts," he said, his voice gentle. "We're offering camp and friendship."

"And lots of s'mores," Red said.

The Witch had never worn a sun hat or felt a warm breeze She giggled for first time in centuries. "Well, I suppose one summer won't hurt. But only if I can join your camp as the official summer spell instructor! I want to contribute too."

And so, summer vacation was saved, and Camp Evergreen had its most magical season yet. The Wicked Witch of the West was the unexpected star. And s'mores were had by all.

Name: _____ # _____

The Wicked Witch of Summer

Characters: Narrator 1, Narrator 2, Wicked Witch of the West, Red Riding Hood, Big Bad Wolf (BBW), Belle, the Beast, Ana, Jack

Narrator 1: In the heart of the Enchanted Forest, where trees whisper secrets and rivers sing symphonies, an unusual chill pervades.

Narrator 2: Despite summer's dawn, the warmth of the sun's embrace is conspicuously absent.

Narrator 1: The culprit? The Wicked Witch of the West, with her frosty heart, has cast a spell to cancel summer vacation.

Wicked Witch of the West: Why would anyone need more than one season? Spring has everything, clean air, rain, and endless chores!

Narrator 2: Meanwhile, in a cozy cottage, a group of friends gathered, dreaming of Camp Evergreen.

Red Riding Hood: This is unbearable. I had plans to master archery!

BBG: And I wanted to share the true art of howling at the moon. It's very misunderstood and not as easy as it looks.

Belle: We can't let the Witch ruin our summer. There has to be a way to break the spell!

The Beast: What if we invite her to camp? She's probably just lonely.

Red: Or we could bring summer to her! Show her what she's missing!

Ana: We have to try something. I need to row. I need to hike. I need to swim. Have any of you tried to swim in Arendelle?

Narrator 1: As they pondered their plan, Jack bounced in, fresh from his latest beanstalk adventure.

Jack: Why so glum chums? And what's with the calendar? Mine's been stuck on Spring for weeks. I'm ready for those endless summer nights.

Ana: It's the Wicked Witch. She's stopped summer.

Belle: We're thinking of inviting her to camp. Maybe she'll catch the summer spirit.

BBG: Look, I've whipped up an invite.

Beast: Did you make that just now?

BBG: Just something I picked up from Grandma. She's a whiz even without a Cricket.

Narrator 2: The crew prepared gifts of summer: sunscreen, insect repellent, sun hats and a portable beach.

Narrator 1: Upon reaching the Witch's castle, they were greeted by a blizzard.

Name: _____ # _____

The Wicked Witch of Summer - page 2

Wicked Witch of the West: Summer's over!

Ana: Nice ice storm. They aren't easy to conjure.

Wicked Witch of the West: Did you just say something nice to me?

Narrator 2: Belle, nudged forward by Jack, presented the invitation to summer camp.

Belle: It's an invitation to summer camp. For you.

Wicked Witch of the West: Me? Why are you being so nice?

The Beast: What do you say? Don't you just love summer?

Wicked Witch of the West: Not particularly or I wouldn't be surrounded by all this ice.

Ana: I'm usually surrounded by ice, but that doesn't mean I don't like to enjoy summer.

Wicked Witch of the West: Will there be s'mores?

Jack: And sun and sand and sailing and campfires and so much more. What'd you say?

Narrator 1: The Witch, intrigued by the gesture and the promise of summer fun, giggled genuinely for the first time in centuries.

Wicked Witch of the West: Well, I suppose one summer won't hurt. But only if I can join your camp as the official summer spell instructor!

Narrator 2: And so, summer vacation was saved, and Camp Evergreen had its most magical season yet.

Narrator 1: With the Wicked Witch of the West as the unexpected star, s'mores were had by all.

Name: _____ # _____

The Wicked Witch of Summer

1. What is the main conflict in the story?
    a. The characters cannot decide on their summer plans.
    b. The Wicked Witch of the West has cast a spell to stop summer.
    c. Red Riding Hood wants to master archery.
    d. BBG wants to teach everyone how to howl at the moon.

2. Which character shows a change in attitude by the end of the story?
    a. The Big Bad Wolf (BBG)
    b. Belle
    c. The Wicked Witch of the West
    d. Jack

3. What literary device is used when the trees whisper secrets and rivers sing symphonies?
    a. Hyperbole
    b. Simile
    c. Personification
    d. Metaphor

4. Why do the characters decide to invite the Wicked Witch to summer camp?
    a. They want to show her what she's missing by not experiencing summer.
    b. They are afraid of her and hope to make peace.
    c. They believe she has never been invited to anything before.
    d. They need her magical powers to help with the camp activities.

5. What theme is best represented by the story?
    a. The importance of mastering a skill
    b. Friendship and understanding can overcome differences.
    c. Summer vacations are essential for personal growth.
    d. Witchcraft and magic are misunderstood arts.

6. Which element of the plot shows the resolution?
    a. The characters planning to break the spell
    b. The confrontation with the Wicked Witch at her castle
    c. The Witch accepting the invitation to summer camp and changing her attitude
    d. The discussion around the fire about missing Camp Evergreen

7. Summarize the story in five to six sentences.

_____
_____
_____
_____
_____
_____

Teacher Page   Name: _____ # _____

The Wicked Witch of Summer

1. What is the main conflict in the story?
    a. The characters cannot decide on their summer plans.
    <u>b. The Wicked Witch of the West has cast a spell to stop summer.</u>
    c. Red Riding Hood wants to master archery.
    d. BBG wants to teach everyone how to howl at the moon.

2. Which character shows a change in attitude by the end of the story?
    a. The Big Bad Wolf (BBG)
    b. Belle
    <u>c. The Wicked Witch of the West</u>
    d. Jack

3. What literary device is used when the trees whisper secrets and rivers sing symphonies?
    a. Hyperbole
    b. Simile
    <u>c. Personification</u>
    d. Metaphor

4. Why do the characters decide to invite the Wicked Witch to summer camp?
    <u>a. They want to show her what she's missing by not experiencing summer.</u>
    b. They are afraid of her and hope to make peace.
    c. They believe she has never been invited to anything before.
    d. They need her magical powers to help with the camp activities.

5. What theme is best represented by the story?
    a. The importance of mastering a skill
    <u>b. Friendship and understanding can overcome differences.</u>
    c. Summer vacations are essential for personal growth.
    d. Witchcraft and magic are misunderstood arts.

6. Which element of the plot shows the resolution?
    a. The characters planning to break the spell
    b. The confrontation with the Wicked Witch at her castle
    <u>c. The Witch accepting the invitation to summer camp and changing her attitude</u>
    d. The discussion around the fire about missing Camp Evergreen

7. Summarize the story in five to six sentences.

   In the Enchanted Forest, the Wicked Witch of the West casts a spell to stop summer, forcing everyone into endless spring cleaning. Red Riding Hood, the Big Bad Wolf (now known as BBG), Belle, the Beast, and Ana are upset because they'll miss their beloved Camp Evergreen. They decide to invite the Witch to camp, hoping to show her the joys of summer and change her mind. Armed with summer essentials and a warm invitation, they brave a blizzard to reach her castle and offer her friendship and a spot at camp. In the end, the Witch is touched by their gesture, agrees to join the camp as the summer spell instructor, and summer vacation is joyfully restored.

Name: _____ # _____

The Wicked Witch of Summer

1. **Inference** - What can be inferred about the Wicked Witch's personality at the beginning of the story, and how does her attitude change by the end?

2. **Theme** - What is the main theme of the story, and how is it conveyed through the characters and plot?

3. **Character Development** - How does the Wicked Witch of the West's character develop throughout the story?

4. **Analyzing Dialogue** - How does the dialogue between the Witch and the other characters contribute to the resolution of the conflict?

5. **Figurative Language** - Identify and explain the use of figurative language in the description of the Enchanted Forest.

Name: _____ # _____

The Wicked Witch of Summer

Inference - What can be inferred about the Wicked Witch's personality at the beginning of the story, and how does her attitude change by the end?

At the beginning, the Wicked Witch of the West appears to be grumpy, isolated, and set in her ways, as shown by her decision to cancel summer vacation and her sarcastic remark about the benefits of spring. By the end, however, her acceptance of the invitation to summer camp and her willingness to become the official summer spell instructor suggest a significant softening of her attitude and a newfound openness to friendship and change. This transformation can be inferred from her initial resistance to the idea of summer and her eventual chuckling and agreement to join the camp activities.

Theme - What is the main theme of the story, and how is it conveyed through the characters and plot?

The main theme of the story is the power of kindness and inclusivity to transform and heal. This theme is conveyed through the actions of Red Riding Hood, BBG, Belle, the Beast, Ana, and Jack as they extend an olive branch to the Wicked Witch by inviting her to summer camp, despite her actions against summer. Their willingness to include someone who is often ostracized and viewed negatively by others, and their efforts to show her the joys of summer and friendship, illustrate how kindness and inclusivity can lead to positive change in individuals and communities.

Character Development - How does the Wicked Witch of the West's character develop throughout the story?

The Wicked Witch of the West's character develops from a villain who casts a spell to cancel summer, highlighting her isolation and bitterness, to a participant in summer camp, indicating her openness to new experiences and community. Her development is marked by her initial skepticism of the group's intentions and her eventual acceptance of their offer, demonstrating a shift from suspicion and solitude to curiosity and a desire for companionship.

Analyzing Dialogue - How does the dialogue between the Witch and the other characters contribute to the resolution of the conflict?

The dialogue plays a crucial role in resolving the conflict. The characters' friendly and inclusive language, their offers of summer camp activities, and their assurances of no ulterior motives gradually break down the Witch's defenses. For example, the Beast's offer of double chocolate s'mores and the mention of various camp activities by Jack serve to entice the Witch and demonstrate the group's genuine desire for her to join them. This dialogue facilitates a shift in the Witch's perspective, leading to the resolution of the conflict as she decides to join the camp.

Figurative Language - Identify and explain the use of figurative language in the description of the Enchanted Forest.

The description of the Enchanted Forest as a place "where trees whisper secrets and rivers sing symphonies" uses personification to give life and magical qualities to the forest. This figurative language creates a vivid, enchanting setting that sets the tone for the story, suggesting a place of mystery and wonder where magical events are possible and emphasizing the story's fairy-tale nature.

Teacher Page

The Wicked Witch of Summer

Theme: The primary theme is the power of community and kindness to transform and overcome barriers. It illustrates how extending a hand in friendship and understanding can change even the coldest of hearts. Additionally, it emphasizes the importance of seasons and the natural cycle, showcasing how diversity in experiences enriches life.

Setting: The story is set a magical "Enchanted Forest," a place where the natural elements have personalities and magic is a part of everyday life. The setting extends from a cozy cottage to the Wicked Witch's icy castle, contrasting the warmth of companionship with the coldness of isolation.

Character Traits

- **The Wicked Witch of the West**: Initially cold-hearted and solitary, believing in the monotony of a single season. Her transformation reveals a capacity for enjoyment and contribution to the community.
- **Red Riding Hood**: Determined and proactive, she's not one to sit idly by when faced with a problem, showing leadership qualities.
- **The Big Bad Wolf (BBG)**: Benevolent and creative, he challenges stereotypes with his gentle nature and artistic talent.
- **Belle**: Optimistic and diplomatic, she plays a key role in extending an olive branch to the Witch, believing in the power of kindness.
- **The Beast**: Thoughtful and sensitive, he suggests inclusive solutions, showing a deep understanding of others' feelings.
- **Ana**: Adventurous and resilient, she brings a practical edge to the group's idealism, emphasizing action.
- **Jack**: Lighthearted and spirited, he brings levity and a sense of adventure to the group.

Main Idea: The story centers around a group of friends from the Enchanted Forest who come together to reverse the Wicked Witch of the West's spell that threatens to eliminate summer. It highlights their journey from planning to action, demonstrating teamwork, creativity, and the willingness to engage with someone who initially seems to be an adversary.

Problem: The central conflict arises from the Wicked Witch of the West's spell that prevents summer from arriving, disrupting the natural cycle and the plans of the forest inhabitants looking forward to summer camp.

Solution: The solution is ingeniously social and emotional rather than confrontational. By inviting the Witch to join their summer camp, offering friendship and showing her the joys of summer, they melt her frosty exterior and convince her to revoke her spell. This not only solves the immediate problem of the eternal spring but also transforms the Witch into a valuable member of their community.

Name: _____ # _____

The Wicked Witch of Summer
Compare and Contrast - Interactive Notebook

Directions: Cut along solid lines, attach at the dashed line. Make a book, one shape on top of the other and attach to your notebook

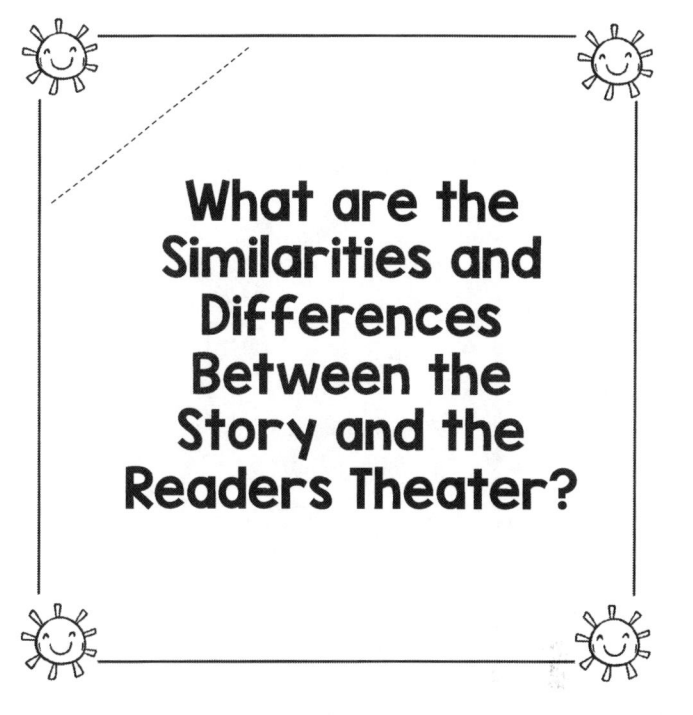

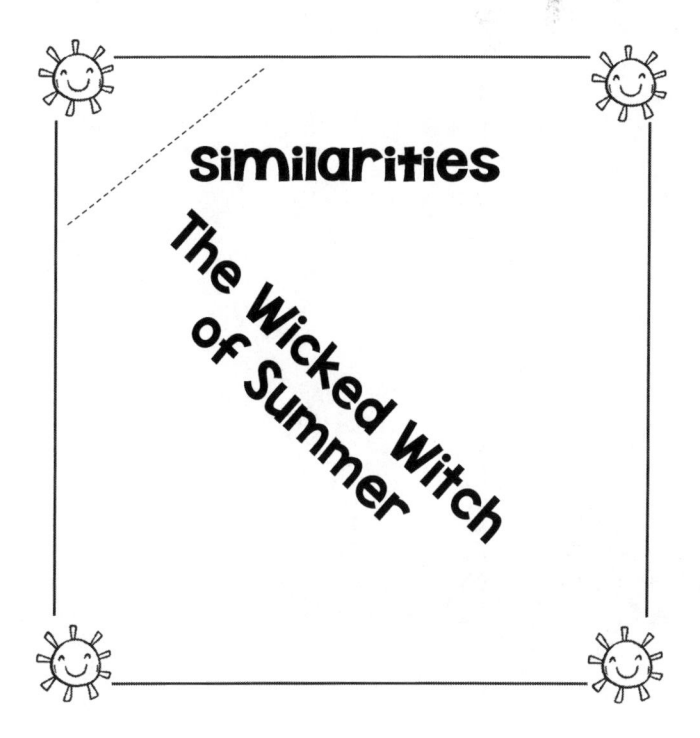

What are the Similarities and Differences Between the Story and the Readers Theater?

Differences
The Wicked Witch of Summer

Similarities
The Wicked Witch of Summer

55

Name: _____ # _____

**The Wicked Witch of Summer
Theme - Interactive Notebook**

Directions: Cut along solid lines, attach at the dashed line. Make a book, one shape on top of the other and attach to your notebook

What is the theme of **The Wicked Witch of Summer**

56

Name: _____ # _____

Teacher Page

**The Wicked Witch of Summer
Theme - Interactive Notebook**

Directions: Cut along solid lines, attach at the dashed line. Make a book, one shape on top of the other and attach to your notebook

What is the theme of **The Wicked Witch of Summer**

The theme of the story highlights the power of community, kindness, and understanding to transform and resolve conflicts. It demonstrates that by coming together and sharing positive experiences, even the most reluctant hearts can be opened to change and joy.

57

Character Traits

Character traits are qualities or characteristics that describe what a person is like. It's how someone behaves and thinks.

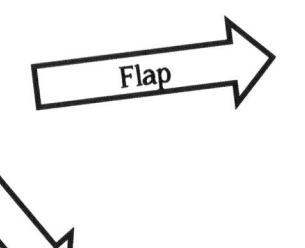

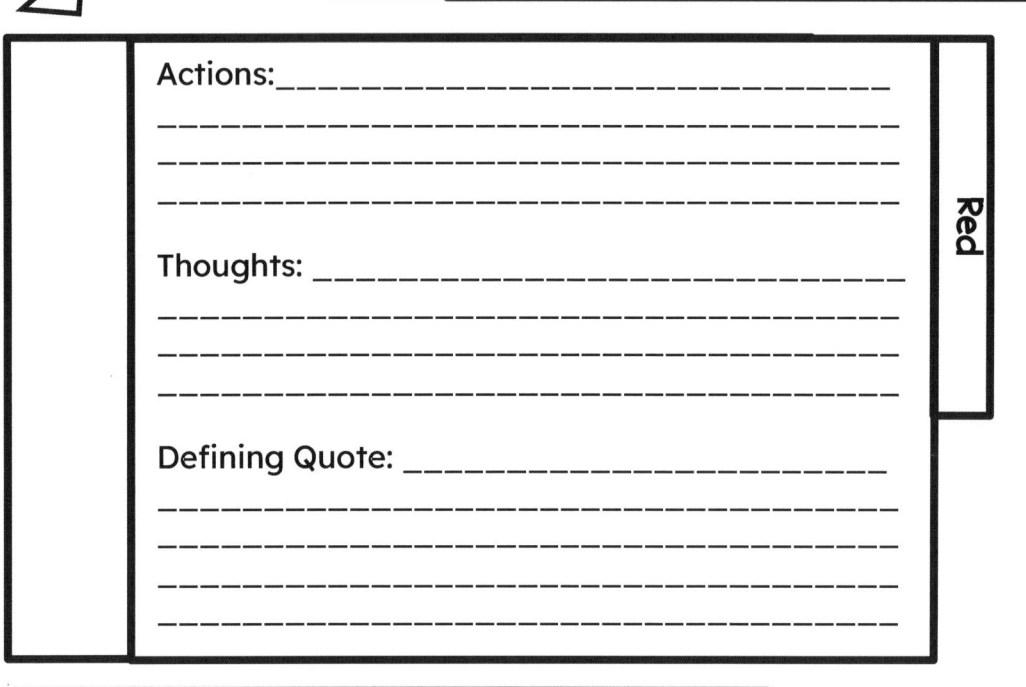

Flap →

↘ Flap

Character Traits
The Wicked Witch of Summer

Actions:_____
_____
_____
_____

Thoughts: _____
_____
_____
_____

Defining Quote: _____
_____
_____
_____
_____

Red

Actions_____
_____
_____
_____

Thoughts: _____
_____
_____
_____

Defining Quote: _____
_____
_____
_____
_____

Belle

Directions: Cut along the outside of the shapes. Glue under the flaps. Glue Box 2 into your notebook. Glue Box one under flap on top and place on top of Box 2. Glue "Character Traits" under flap to create a cover for the pages on top.

Character Traits

Character traits are qualities or characteristics that describe what a person is like. It's how someone behaves and thinks.

Flap →

↓ Flap

Character Traits
The Wicked Witch of Summer

Actions:_____
_____
_____
_____

Thoughts: _____
_____
_____
_____

Defining Quote: _____
_____
_____
_____
_____

Wicked Witch

Actions_____
_____
_____
_____

Thoughts: _____
_____
_____
_____

Defining Quote: _____
_____
_____
_____
_____

Jack

Directions: Cut along the outside of the shapes. Glue under the flaps. Glue Box 2 into your notebook. Glue Box one under flap on top and place on top of Box 2. Glue "Character Traits" under flap to create a cover for the pages on top.

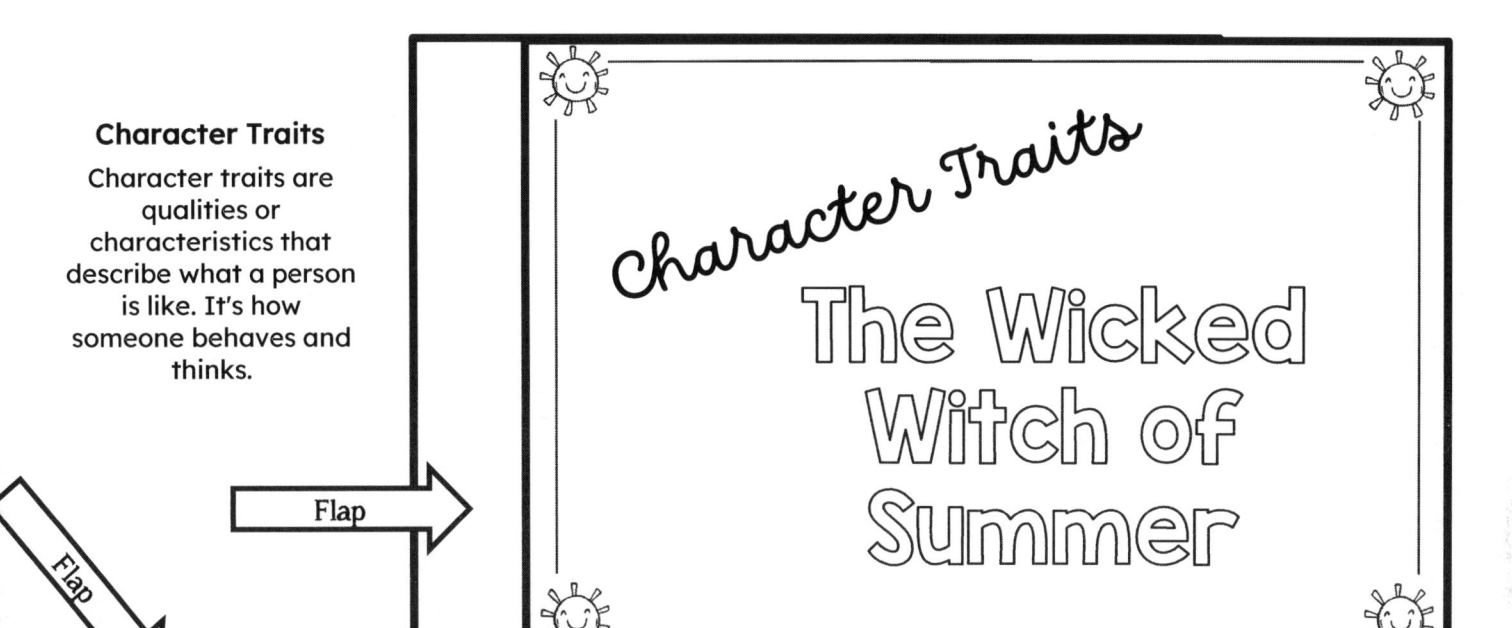

59

Name: _____ # _____

Making Inferences RL.1

The Wicked Witch of Summer - Theme

Directions: Cut along the outside of the shapes. Glue under the flap and attach it to your notebook to write under the flap. Choose a quote from the story. Write it under the "What Was Said" flap. Write what you think the quote means, or implies, under the "What It Implies" flap. What can you infer from your selected quote.

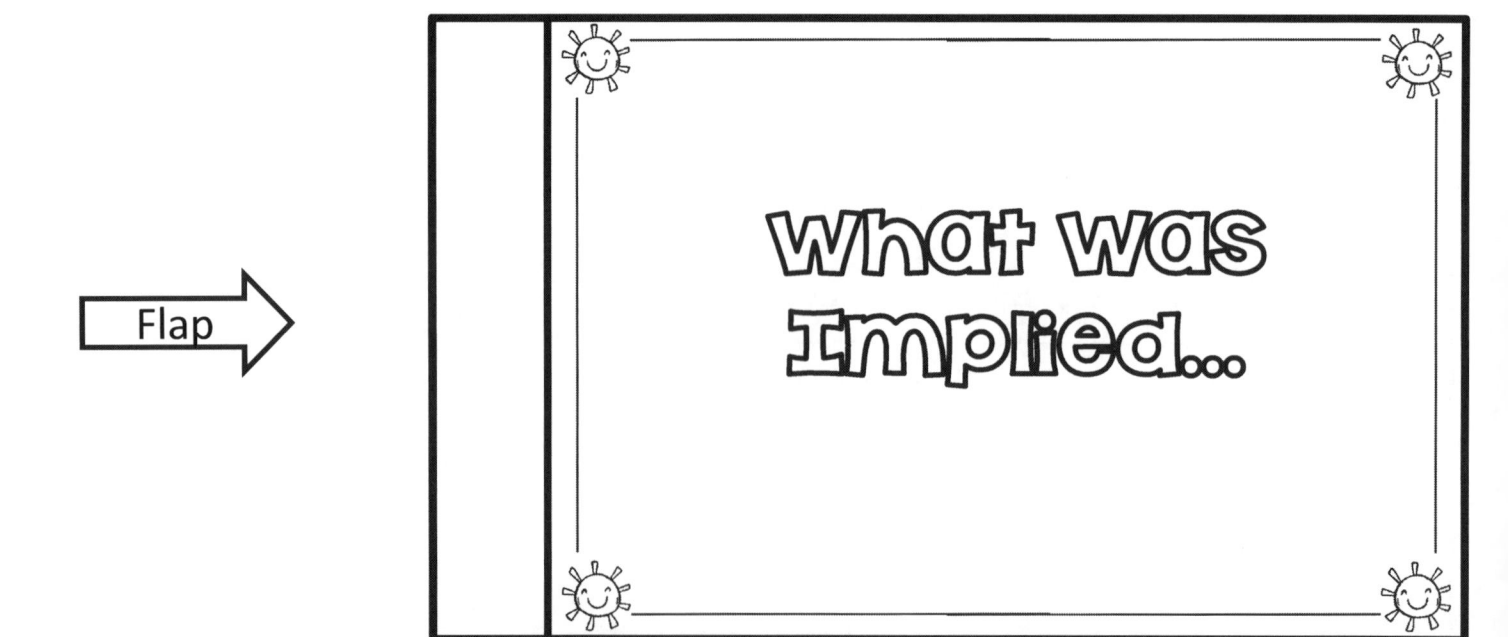

Flap ➡

What was said...

Flap ➡

What was Implied...

Inference: An inference is a conclusion drawn from evidence from your reading, your thoughts and what you know about life and events.

Name: _____ # _____

Making Inferences RL 1

The Wicked Witch of Summer

Directions: Cut on the solid lines. Fold on the dotted lines. Glue or tape the center to your notebook. Answer the questions under the flaps.

Inference: An inference is a conclusion drawn from evidence in your reading, your thoughts and what you know about life and events.

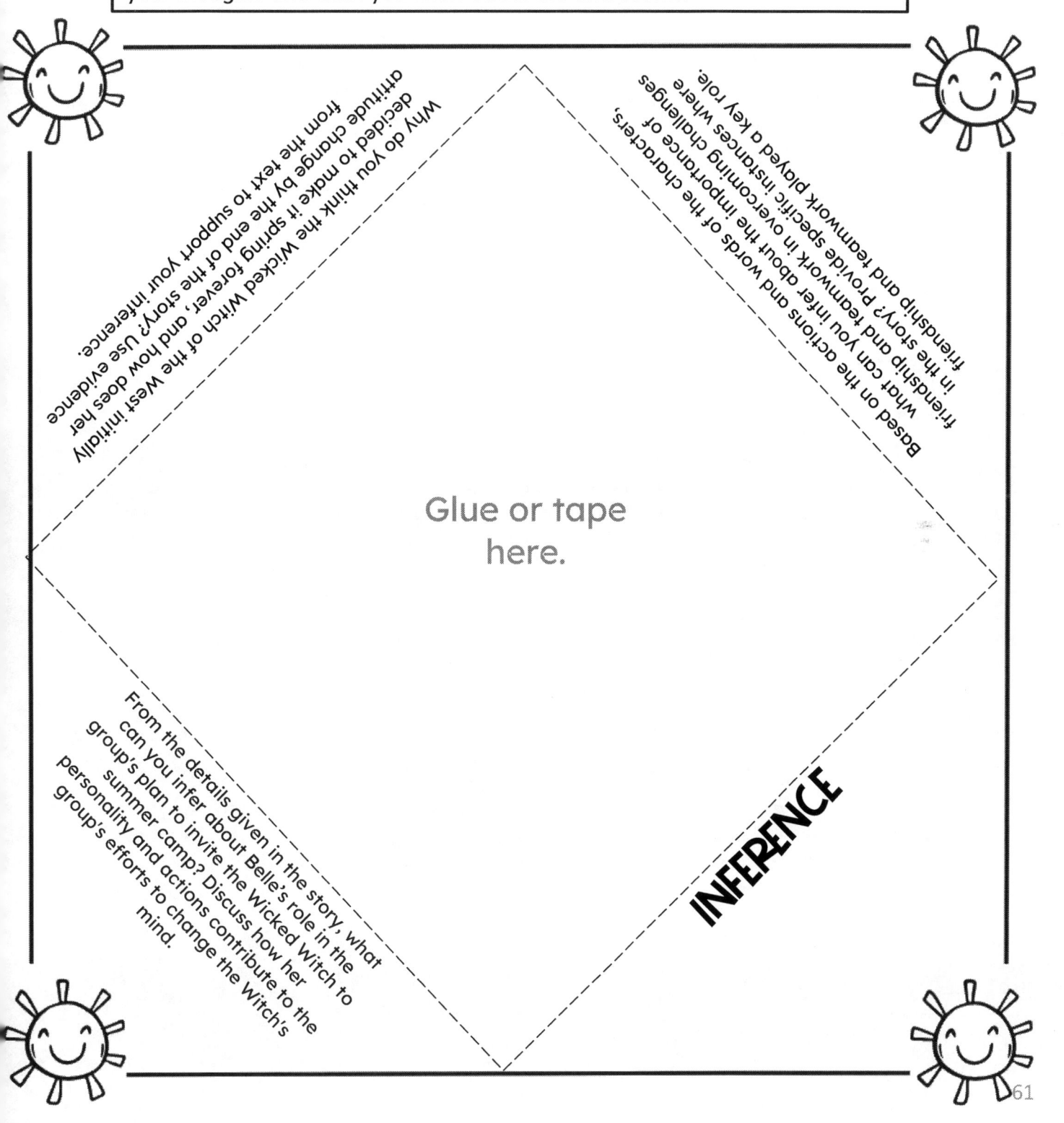

Why do you think the Wicked Witch of the West initially decided to make it spring forever, and how does her attitude change by the end of the story? Use evidence from the text to support your inference.

Based on the actions and words of the characters, what can you infer about the importance of friendship and teamwork in overcoming challenges in the story? Provide specific instances where friendship and teamwork played a key role.

Glue or tape here.

From the details given in the story, what can you infer about Belle's role in the group's plan to invite the Wicked Witch to summer camp? Discuss how her personality and actions contribute to the group's efforts to change the Witch's mind.

INFERENCE

Teacher Page

Name: _____ # _____

Making Inferences RL I

The Wicked Witch of Summer

Directions: Cut on the solid lines. Fold on the dotted lines. Glue or tape the center to your notebook. Answer the questions under the flaps.

> **Inference:** An inference is a conclusion drawn from evidence in your reading, your thoughts and what you know about life and events.

Question 1: Why do you think the Wicked Witch of the West decided to make it spring forever, and how does her attitude change by the end of the story? Use evidence from the text to support your inference.

Inferred Answer The Wicked Witch of the West probably made it spring forever because she's all about that clean air and getting chores done. She's like, "Why need more than one season when you've got all this?" But by the end, after she hangs with the camp crew and sees all the fun summer stuff, her vibe totally flips. She even starts laughing for real, which sounds like she hadn't done in forever. It's like she finally got that there's more to life than just being stuck on repeat with spring cleaning.

Question 2: Based on the actions and words of the characters, what can you infer about the importance of friendship and teamwork in overcoming challenges in the story? Provide specific instances where friendship and teamwork played a key role.

Inferred Answer: Friendship and teamwork are mega important in this story. Like, when they all decide to tackle the Witch's eternal spring problem, they each bring something cool to the table. BBG's crafting skills, Ana's magical summer breeze, and Belle's bravery in facing the Witch show that when friends work together, they can make even the grumpiest Witch have a change of heart. It's like they all have their own superpowers, but together, they're unstoppable.

Question 3: From the details given in the story, what can you infer about Belle's role in the group's plan to invite the Wicked Witch to summer camp? Discuss how her personality and actions contribute to the group's efforts to change the Witch's mind.

Inferred Answer: Belle's role in getting the Witch to come to camp is pretty key. She's like the peace envoy, the one who's got enough chill and kindness to not get turned into a frog when she hands over the invite. Belle being all diplomatic and brave enough to walk into what's basically a blizzard shows she's got this way of making peace and bringing people together. Her doing this wasn't just about being nice; it was strategic, showing she knew how to reach out and maybe change the Witch's mind with a mix of courage and a big heart.

INFERENCE

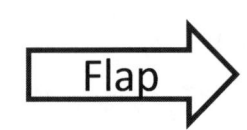

Name: _____ # _____

Key Ideas and Details RL.1: Cite textual evidence to support analysis of text, both inferential and explicit.

Directions: Cut along the outside of the shapes. Glue under the flap and attach to write under the flap. Answer the question under the flap.

The Wicked Witch of Summer

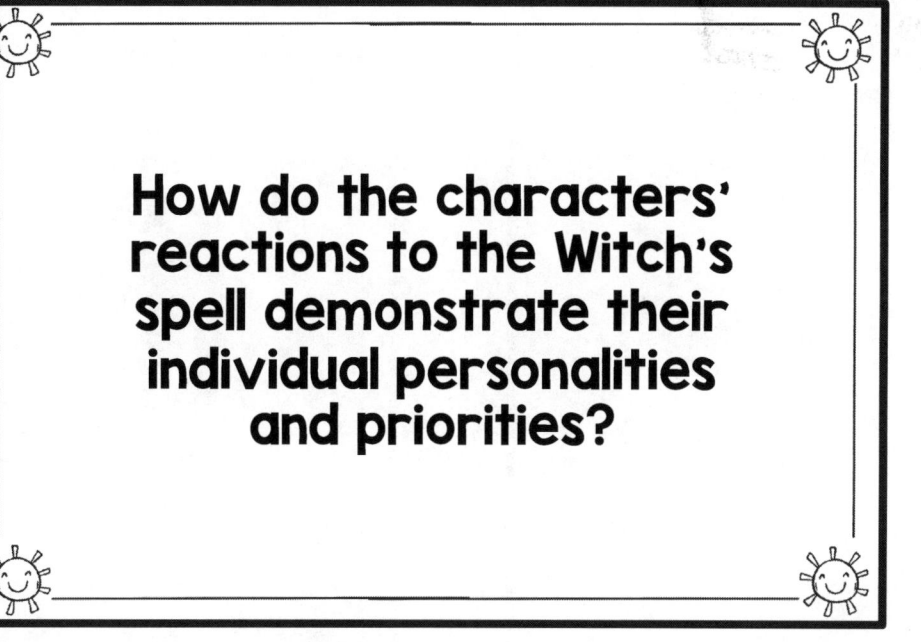

Flap →

What parts of the story show that the Wicked Witch of the West didn't mean to be completely mean by making it spring all the time? Use details from the story to back up your answer.

Flap →

How do the characters' reactions to the Witch's spell demonstrate their individual personalities and priorities?

63

Name: _____ # _____

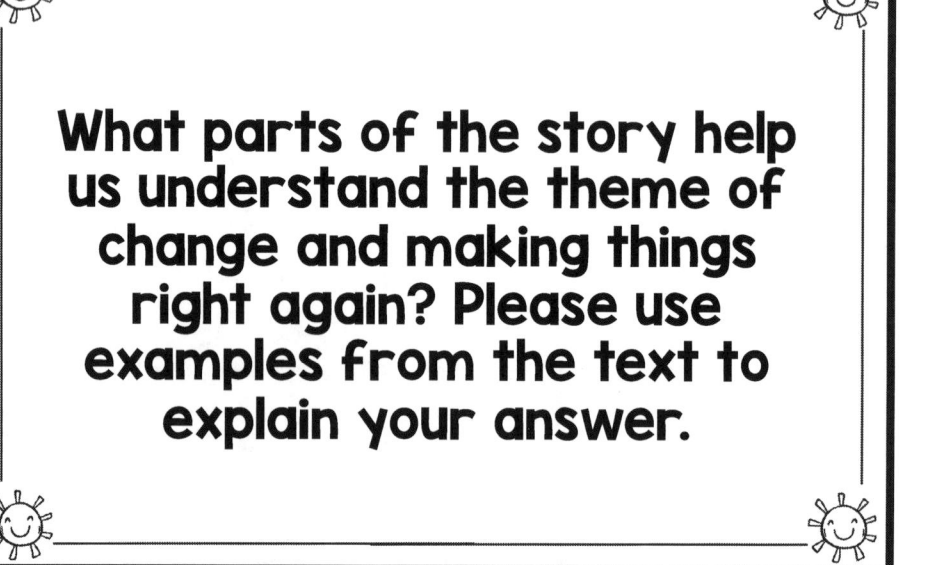

Key Ideas and Details RL.1: Cite textual evidence to support analysis of text, both inferential and explicit.

Directions: Cut along the outside of the shapes. Glue under the flap and attach to write under the flap. Answer the question under the flap.

The Wicked Witch of Summer

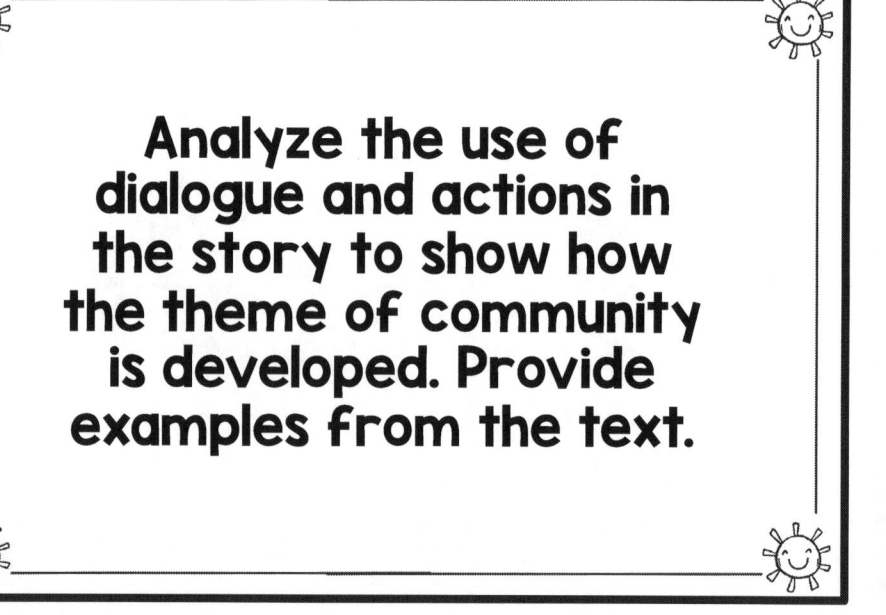

Flap →

What parts of the story help us understand the theme of change and making things right again? Please use examples from the text to explain your answer.

Flap →

Analyze the use of dialogue and actions in the story to show how the theme of community is developed. Provide examples from the text.

Teacher Page

Key Ideas and Details RL.1: Cite textual evidence to support analysis of text, both inferential and explicit.

Question 1: What parts of the story show that the Wicked Witch of the West didn't mean to be completely mean by making it spring all the time? Use details from the story to back up your answer.

Answer Guidance: Teachers should guide students to recognize that the Witch's motivation behind making it spring forever was not to harm the inhabitants of the Enchanted Forest, but rather based on her own perspective of what's beneficial (e.g., "clean air, rain, and endless chores"). Students should cite her initial reasoning for the spell as evidence of her intentions not being entirely malicious, but perhaps misguided or one-dimensional.

Question 2: How do the characters' reactions to the Witch's spell demonstrate their individual personalities and priorities?

Answer Guidance: Encourage students to examine each character's response to the spell. For example, Red Riding Hood's frustration about missing out on archery, BBG's disappointment over not sharing the art of howling, and Ana's longing for summer activities unique to warmer seasons. These reactions not only highlight their individual interests but also their resilience in facing adversity. Students should provide specific examples from the text that illustrate these character traits.

Question 3: What parts of the story help us understand the theme of change and making things right again? Please use examples from the text to explain your answer.

Answer Guidance: Students should focus on the development of the Wicked Witch's character, from casting a spell for eternal spring to accepting the invitation to summer camp and even laughing genuinely. Key moments include her curiosity about the summer camp activities, the change in her demeanor upon receiving kindness from the group, and her final acceptance to join the camp as the official summer spell instructor. This progression shows her transformation and redemption, underlining the story's theme.

Question 4: Analyze the use of dialogue and actions in the story to show how the theme of community is developed. Provide examples from the text.

Answer Guidance: Guide students to notice how dialogue and actions between characters build the theme of community. Examples include the collaborative planning to invite the Witch to summer camp, Belle's diplomatic role, and the collective effort to demonstrate the joys of summer to the Witch. The dialogue that ensues during these plans, especially the inclusive and optimistic tones, alongside actions like crafting invitations and assembling summer essentials, serve to underscore the importance of community in overcoming obstacles. Encourage students to provide specific dialogue excerpts and descriptions of actions that highlight this theme.

Name: _____ # _____

Key Ideas and Detail RL.2 - Theme Development

The Wicked Witch of Summer

Theme The Message. A theme is the moral or lesson of a story - it is the underlying meaning. **Analyze how the theme is developed throughout the story.**

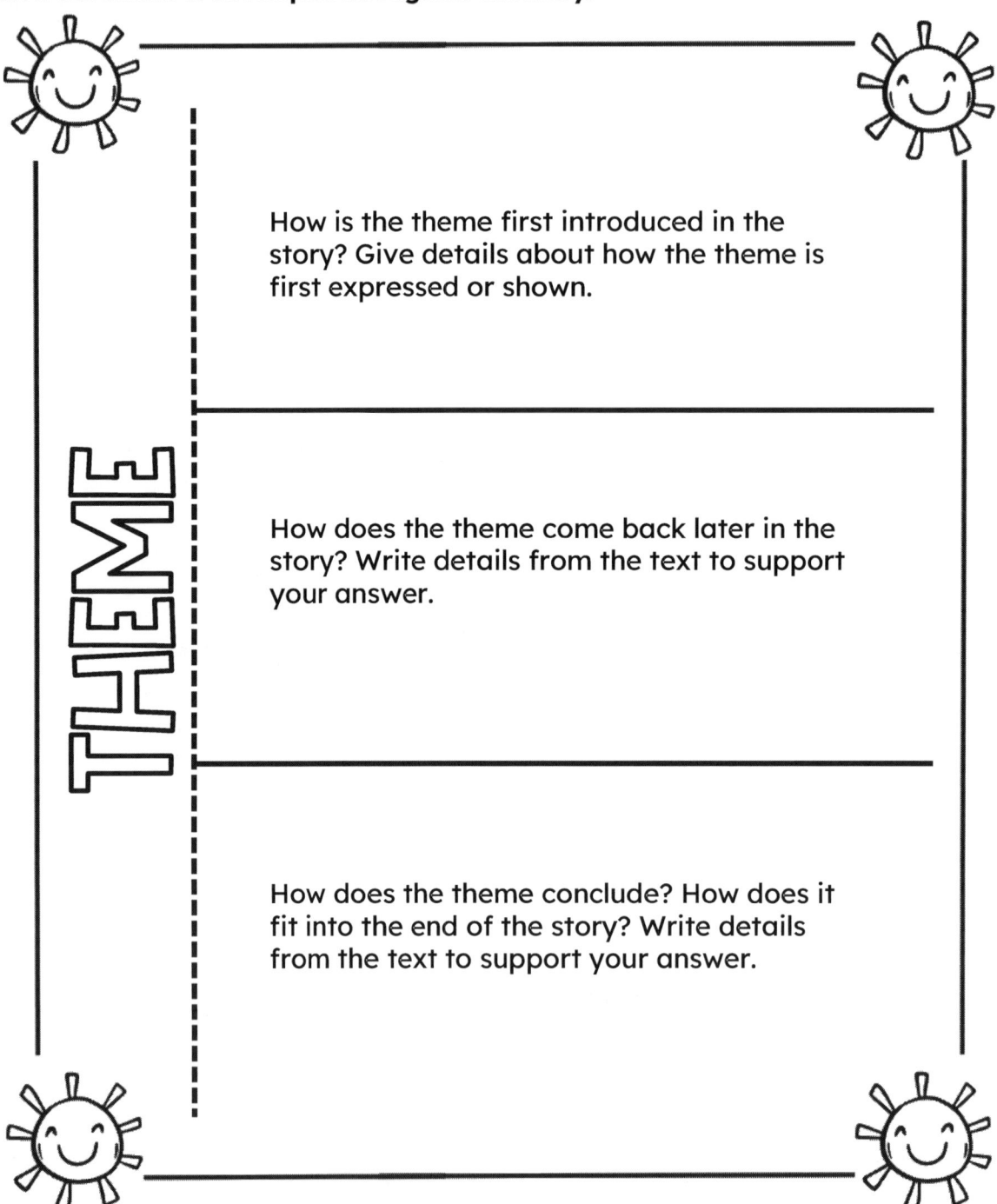

THEME

How is the theme first introduced in the story? Give details about how the theme is first expressed or shown.

How does the theme come back later in the story? Write details from the text to support your answer.

How does the theme conclude? How does it fit into the end of the story? Write details from the text to support your answer.

Directions: Cut along the solid lines. Fold along the dotted lines. Write your answer under the flaps.

Teacher Page Name: _____ # _____

Key Ideas and Detail RL.2 - Theme Development

The Wicked Witch of Summer

Theme <u>The Message</u>. A theme is the moral or lesson of a story – it is the underlying meaning. **Analyze how the theme is developed throughout the story.**

THEME

The story begins by showing us a magical forest that's stuck in spring because of a spell by the Wicked Witch of the West. This part of the story introduces the main idea that things need to change and that working together might be the way to do it. The forest being stuck in spring hints that something's not right and that the characters will need to find a way to bring back summer, showing us that change is necessary and that teamwork might help achieve it.

As the story goes on, we see the characters, like Red Riding Hood, the Big Bad Wolf (who's actually nice and called BBG), Belle, the Beast, and Ana, all coming up with a plan to invite the Witch to a summer camp. This part shows the theme again because they decide to work together to solve the problem. They all think that being nice and showing the Witch how great summer can be might make her change her mind. This shows that working together and being kind are powerful ways to make good changes happen.

In the end, the theme is shown when the Witch decides to end the spell and let summer come back because she enjoyed the company and the fun activities of summer camp. She even laughs for real, which she hasn't done in a very long time, and wants to be part of the camp as a teacher. This ending shows us that the characters' plan to work together and be kind really worked. It changed the Witch's mind and brought back summer. This fits perfectly with the story's message that kindness and teamwork can lead to big, positive changes, even changing someone's heart.

Directions: Cut along the solid lines. Fold along the dotted lines. Write your answer under the flaps.

Name: _____ # _____

Key Ideas and Detail RL.2 - Sequence of Events

Directions: Cut along the solid lines. Fold along the dotted lines. Write your answer under the flaps.

The Wicked Witch of Summer

The Wicked Witch of Summer

In the Beginning,

Then,

Lastly,

Key Ideas and Detail RL.6 - Point of View
Analyzing the Author's Attitude

Directions: Cut along the solid lines. Fold along the dotted lines. Write your answer under the flaps.

Analyze how the writer's attitude influences the beliefs of the characters.

The Wicked Witch of Summer

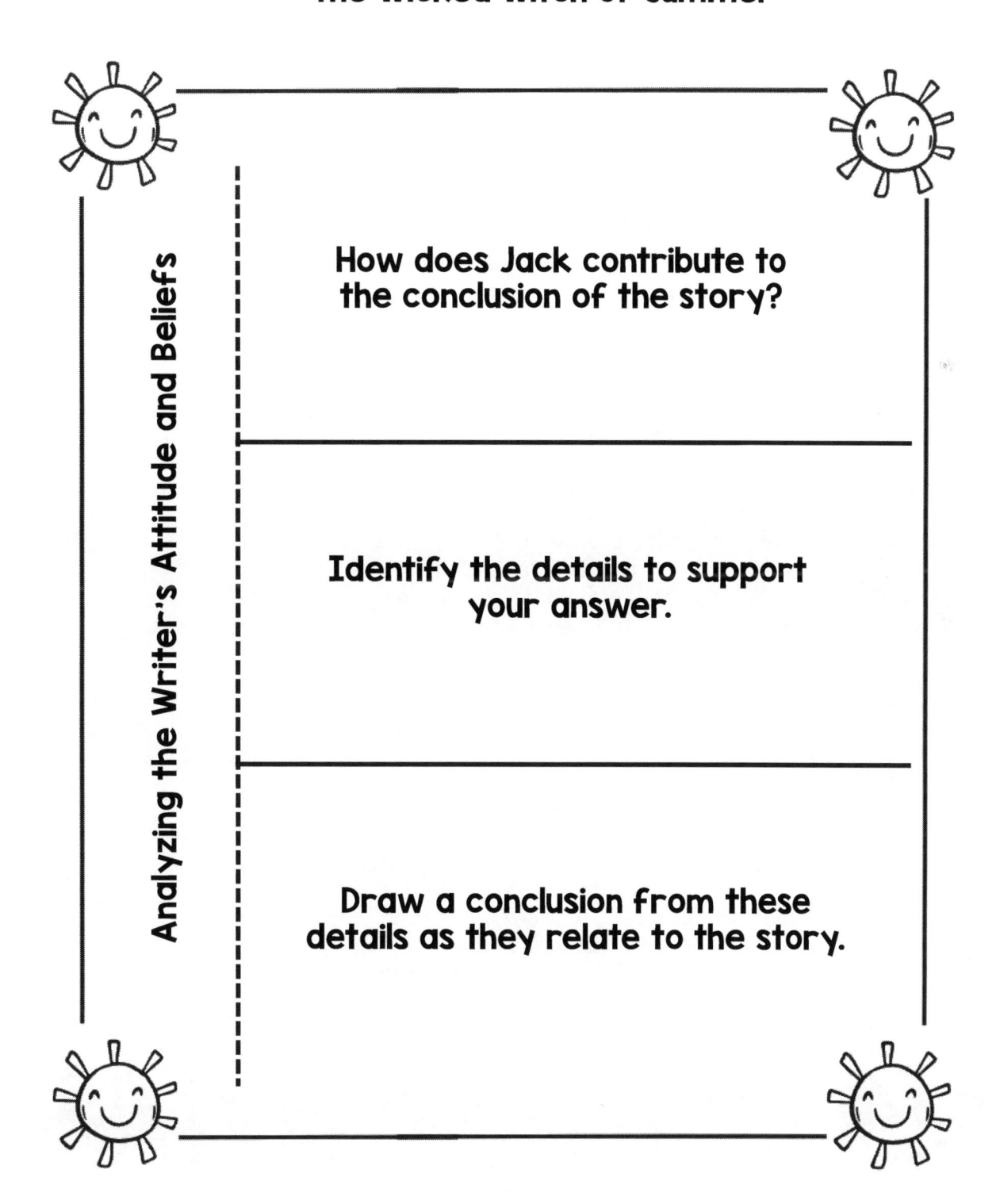

Analyzing the Writer's Attitude and Beliefs

How does Jack contribute to the conclusion of the story?

Identify the details to support your answer.

Draw a conclusion from these details as they relate to the story.

Teacher Page   Name: _____ # _____

Key Ideas and Detail RL.6 - Point of View
Analyzing the Author's Attitude

Directions: Cut along the solid lines. Fold along the dotted lines. Write your answer under the flaps.

Analyze how the writer's attitude influences the beliefs of the characters.

The Wicked Witch of Summer

Analyzing the Writer's Attitude and Beliefs

Jack helps out in the ending of the story in a cool but quiet way. He doesn't fix everything by himself, but he does something important. When he shows up and asks why everyone is so down, it kind of lights up the mood and reminds everyone why they're trying to fix the problem with the Witch and the weird weather. Plus, when he talks about missing summer nights, it makes everyone remember what they're missing and makes them want to fix things even more.

Jack also gets in on the plan to invite the Witch to summer camp. Even though he ends up saying he can't go give her the invite because of a funny past problem with a golden goose, him just being there and liking the idea of the invitation helps everyone feel good about their plan.

So, what we can learn from what Jack does is pretty cool. Even though he doesn't do the big stuff, he still helps a lot. His being there makes everyone feel better and keeps them going on their plan to bring back summer. It shows that everyone in a group has something they can do to help, even if they're not the one in the spotlight. It's like, every bit of help counts when friends are working together to fix a problem.

Name: _____   Partner: _____

The Wicked Witch of Summer
Think - Pair - Share

Read "The Wicked Witch of Summer."

Part 1: Think (Individual Work) – Answer the questions.

Characters: List the main characters and their traits. _____
_____
_____

Plot: Summarize the key events in the story. _____
_____
_____
_____

Themes: Identify the themes or moral lessons in the story. _____
_____
_____
_____

Part 2: Pair (Discussion with a Partner)
Questions for Discussion:
- What makes the characters unique?
- How do they solve the crisis?
- How does the setting contribute to the story?
- What are some real-life lessons that can be learned from this story?

Problem-Solving: Brainstorm ideas on how you could change or add to the story to make it more interesting.
_____
_____
_____
_____
_____
_____

Part 3: Be Prepared to Share Out

One new idea you heard during the discussion: _____
_____
_____
_____

One point you agreed/disagreed with and why: _____
_____
_____
_____

Summer Jobs, Captain Hook and a Dragon

Summer Jobs, Captain Hook and a Dragon 1.0

Once upon an un-mowed lawn, a unique business idea sprouted because a few fairy tale teens needed to earn money for next year's school clothes.

"This dress has been around for centuries," Cinderella said. "It's looking worse for wear."

"And have you noticed how much alike my dress is to Alice's?" Belle remarked. "Think about it. I'm wearing the same clothes as Alice-in-Wonderland. I'm ready for a change."

"We're cool. We're smart. Let's put our entrepreneur hats together and see what we can come up with," Rapunzel agreed.

"I have the best idea ever," Aladdin's interjected. "Let's mow lawns."

"What a great idea," Prince Eric said.

"With Genie's magic and our combined skills, we'll have the best lawns this side of Neverland!" he said with a confidence that could convince even the most skeptical of villains.

The Genie, ever eager to please, boasted, "And for my first trick—uh, business strategy—I'll conjure the ultimate lawn mower. Behold, the 'Grass Master 3000'!" His hands sparkled with magic, but everyone knew the real magic was in his dramatic flair.

Rapunzel, adjusting a sun hat over her famous locks, added, "And my hair can...uh, well, I'll handle the customer service!" She was always looking to be more than just her hair.

Their enterprise, "Grass Happens," was a hit, until Captain Hook, reborn as Captain Cook, and his new dragon crashed their party.

"Arrr, me hearties. Think ye can control the lawn market? Me dragon and I will scorch ye out of business!" Captain Cook threatened, his dragon belching a small puff of smoke in agreement, albeit more interested in its own tail.

Quick thinkers Hansel and Gretel proposed a solution. "Let's challenge them to a lawn-off. May the best team win!" they said, their faces alight with mischief honed from their breadcrumb days.

The day of the competition arrived with much anticipation, then things fell apart.

The competition was a mess. Captain Cook's dragon, instead of mowing, set a bush ablaze, while the Genie's "Grass Master 3000" turned the grass into a disco floor rather than a clean-cut lawn.

Prince Eric laughed, saying, "This wasn't the adventure I expected, but at least it's not another sea witch."

As the townsfolk gathered, entertained by the chaos, Aladdin saw an opportunity. "What say you, Captain? Perhaps there's room in this town for both of us. Just not manicuring yards," he offered, a hand extended in peace.

Name: _____ # _____

Summer Jobs, Captain Hook and a Dragon 1.0 - page 2

Captain Cook, momentarily baffled and scratching his head, found the idea appealing. "Arr, perhaps we should join forces. The crowd seems to love us. What be the name of this venture?" he asked, already warming to the idea of partnership over rivalry.

Rapunzel, with a creative spark in her eye, suggested, "Grass Happens & Dragon Trims!" It was a name that promised not just lawn care, but a spectacle.

And so, they did. They combined their talents and turned lawn care into a performance art, touring the kingdom and spreading joy (and well-manicured lawns) everywhere. They discovered that while competition is thrilling, collaboration brings not only success but also joy and friendship – and a few singed lawns.

Their story became one of unexpected alliances, proving that sometimes, the best business partners come from the most unlikely of friendships.

And they all mowed happily ever after.

Name: _____ # _____

Summer Jobs, Captain Hook and a Dragon 1.0

1. Why did the characters decide to start a lawn mowing business?
    a. They were passionate about gardening.
    b. They needed money for school clothes.
    c. Genie wanted to use his new lawn mower.
    d. They wanted to compete with Captain Cook.

2. What was unique about the lawn mower used in their business?
    a. It was pulled by dragons.
    b. It could mow the lawn by itself.
    c. It turned the grass into a disco floor.
    d. It was powered by magic.

3. How did Rapunzel contribute to the business?
    a. By using her hair to cut the grass.
    b. By handling customer service.
    c. By conjuring magical tools.
    d. By providing the initial business idea.

4. What problem did Captain Cook pose to the lawn mowing business?
    a. He threatened to take over their business.
    b. His dragon kept eating the grass.
    c. He wanted them to pay him protection money.
    d. His dragon set a bush on fire.

5. What was the outcome of the competition between the characters and Captain Cook?
    a. The characters won easily.
    b. Captain Cook and his dragon won.
    c. It ended in a mess with no clear winner.
    d. They decided not to compete after all.

6. How did the story resolve the conflict between the characters and Captain Cook?
    a. By agreeing to merge their businesses.
    b. Through a magical intervention by Genie.
    c. Captain Cook was scared away by the townsfolk.
    d. They all decided to quit the lawn care business.

7. Summarize the story in five to six sentences.

_____
_____
_____
_____
_____
_____

Teacher Page   Name: _____ # _____

Summer Jobs, Captain Hook and a Dragon 1.0

1. Why did the characters decide to start a lawn mowing business?
   a. They were passionate about gardening.
   <u>b. They needed money for school clothes.</u>
   c. Genie wanted to use his new lawn mower.
   d. They wanted to compete with Captain Cook.

2. What was unique about the lawn mower used in their business?
   a. It was pulled by dragons.
   b. It could mow the lawn by itself.
   c. It turned the grass into a disco floor.
   <u>d. It was powered by magic.</u>

3. How did Rapunzel contribute to the business?
   a. By using her hair to cut the grass.
   <u>b. By handling customer service.</u>
   c. By conjuring magical tools.
   d. By providing the initial business idea.

4. What problem did Captain Cook pose to the lawn mowing business?
   <u>a. He threatened to take over their business.</u>
   b. His dragon kept eating the grass.
   c. He wanted them to pay him protection money.
   d. His dragon set a bush on fire.

5. What was the outcome of the competition between the characters and Captain Cook?
   a. The characters won easily.
   b. Captain Cook and his dragon won.
   <u>c. It ended in a mess with no clear winner.</u>
   d. They decided not to compete after all.

6. How did the story resolve the conflict between the characters and Captain Cook?
   <u>a. By agreeing to merge their businesses.</u>
   b. Through a magical intervention by Genie.
   c. Captain Cook was scared away by the townsfolk.
   d. They all decided to quit the lawn care business.

7. Summarize the story in five to six sentences.

In Fairytale Land, a group of fairy tale characters, including Cinderella, Belle, Rapunzel, Aladdin, and Prince Eric, decided to start a lawn mowing business named "Grass Happens" to earn money for school clothes. Using Genie's magic to power the "Grass Master 3000," their venture was initially successful. However, their business faced competition when Captain Cook (formerly Captain Hook) and his grass-trimming dragon threatened to take over the lawn market. Hansel and Gretel suggested a "lawn-off" to settle the rivalry, which ended in a chaotic but entertaining disaster, with no clear winner. Seeing an opportunity in the chaos, Aladdin proposed a partnership with Captain Cook, leading to the creation of "Grass Happens & Dragon Trims," combining their talents to make lawn care a performance art. Their successful collaboration turned competition into friendship and showed that teamwork and creativity could lead to unexpected and joyous outcomes, ending their story with the lesson that the best partnerships can come from unlikely sources.

Summer Jobs, Captain Hook and a Dragon

Once upon a time a group of fairy tale characters got together. They were going to start a business. It was Aladdin's idea.

"I need cash for school clothes," Aladdin said.

"Me too," Cinderella chimed in. "This dress has seen better days!"

"At least you two don't look like Alice-in-Wonderland all the time" Belle muttered.

The three called a meeting. Genie was there. Genie was always looking for something to do post-lamp life. Rapunzel was also there. Rapunzel was tired of her tower. It had a lift now. Easy up. Easy down. Not nearly as fun. Prince Eric was there too. Prince Eric was always up for a land adventure. To round the team were Hansel and Gretel.

Their business idea? A high-tech lawn mowing service. They'd call it "Grass Happens." They'd use Genie's magical mowing app for instant mowing success. The team was unstoppable. Or so they thought. Then Captain Hook, reinvented as Captain Cook, entered the scene. With him with him was his new dragon. Who, apart from breathing fire, could also trim grass super fast.

"This summer will be a bust if I don't make enough for a Dyson. These locks have become unmanageable," Rapunzel said

"Hook or Cook or whatever he wants to be called is killing our business. The dragon's a freak show. It's a train wreck people just have to see," Prince Eric said.

Quick thinkers Hansel and Gretel proposed a solution. "Let's challenge them to a lawn-off. May the best team win!" they said, their faces alight with mischief honed from their breadcrumb days.

"Splendid idea," Genie beamed. "I should have thought of it myself. The winner gets all the tomatoes."

"What'd you say Cook?" Hansel called across the street.

"A lawn off. Winner takes all," Gretel smiled.

A flash of light appeared as a tiny bell sounded.

"Tink!" called Rapunzel. They were friends from Rapunzel's days in the tower. Tink visited Rapunzel often. Both loved a good game of rummy.

"I'll judge," Tink said. "We meet at dawn. May the best team win."

It was chaos. Captain Cook's dragon didn't mow. It set bushes on fire. And Genie's "Grass Master 3000?" It turned the grass into a disco floor rather than cutting it.

Prince Eric had to laugh. "This wasn't what I expected. At least there's no sea witch."

Summer Jobs, Captain Hook and a Dragon - page 2

People came from far and wide to watch the craziness. They loved the show. Aladdin saw dollar signs. "What say you, Captain? Think there's room in this town for both of us? We can entertain as we mow. Charge for the lawns and for the show."

Captain Cook scratched his head. "Hm." Then a smirk formed on his lips. "Arr, perhaps we can join forces. A flashy suit like mine begs to be seen. What be the name of this venture?" he asked, warming to the idea of partnership over rivalry.

"Grass Happens & Dragons Flame!" Rapunzel said.

"Catchy," Cook said.

"I like it," Genie smiled. "Grass Happens & Dragons Flame it is."

And so, they did. They combined their talents and turned lawn care into a performance art, touring the kingdom and spreading joy (and well-manicured lawns) everywhere. Through it all, they found that working together brings not only success but also joy and friendship.

Their story became one of unexpected friendships, proving that sometimes, the best business partners come from the most unlikely of people.

And they all mowed happily ever after.

Name: _____ # _____

Summer Jobs, Captain Hook and a Dragon 2.0

1. Why did Aladdin want to start a business?
    a. He wanted to buy a new lamp.
    b. He needed money for school clothes.
    c. He was bored and wanted something to do.
    d. He wanted to impress Genie.

2. What was special about Genie's lawn mower?
    a. It could fly.
    b. It was very quiet.
    c. It mowed lawns using a magical app.
    d. It was powered by sunlight.

3. What problem did Captain Cook cause for the business?
    a. He stole their lawn mower.
    b. His dragon scared away their customers.
    c. He made fun of their business name.
    d. He was competing with them with his dragon.

4. How did Hansel and Gretel suggest solving the problem with Captain Cook?
    a. By asking for help from Tink.
    b. By challenging him to a lawn mowing competition.
    c. By challenging him to a baking contest.
    d. By running away.

5. What happened during the lawn mowing competition?
    a. Captain Cook's dragon mowed all the lawns perfectly.
    b. Genie's lawn mower worked perfectly, and they won.
    c. It turned chaotic, with fires and a disco floor, but people enjoyed it.
    d. It was cancelled because of rain.

6. What was the final decision made by Aladdin and Captain Cook?
    a. To continue competing against each other.
    b. To stop mowing lawns altogether.
    c. To apologize to the town for the chaos.
    d. To join forces and combine their businesses.

7. Summarize the story in five to six sentences.

_____
_____
_____
_____
_____
_____

Teacher Page   Name: _____ # _____

Summer Jobs, Captain Hook and a Dragon 2.0

1. Why did Aladdin want to start a business?
   a. He wanted to buy a new lamp.
   <u>b. He needed money for school clothes.</u>
   c. He was bored and wanted something to do.
   d. He wanted to impress Genie.

2. What was special about Genie's lawn mower?
   a. It could fly.
   b. It was very quiet.
   <u>c. It mowed lawns using a magical app.</u>
   d. It was powered by sunlight.

3. What problem did Captain Cook cause for the business?
   a. He stole their lawn mower.
   b. His dragon scared away their customers.
   c. He made fun of their business name.
   <u>d. He was competing with them with his dragon.</u>

4. How did Hansel and Gretel suggest solving the problem with Captain Cook?
   a. By asking for help from Tink.
   <u>b. By challenging him to a lawn mowing competition.</u>
   c. By challenging him to a baking contest.
   d. By running away.

5. What happened during the lawn mowing competition?
   a. Captain Cook's dragon mowed all the lawns perfectly.
   b. Genie's lawn mower worked perfectly, and they won.
   <u>c. It turned chaotic, with fires and a disco floor, but people enjoyed it.</u>
   d. It was cancelled because of rain.

6. What was the final decision made by Aladdin and Captain Cook?
   a. To continue competing against each other.
   b. To stop mowing lawns altogether.
   c. To apologize to the town for the chaos.
   <u>d. To join forces and combine their businesses.</u>

7. Summarize the story in five to six sentences.

Aladdin and his fairy tale friends started a lawn mowing business called "Grass Happens" to earn money for school clothes, utilizing Genie's magical mowing app. Their unique venture faced competition when Captain Cook, with his grass-trimming dragon, entered the scene, threatening their business. Hansel and Gretel suggested a lawn-off to settle the rivalry, which turned into a chaotic but entertaining spectacle with no clear winner. Seeing the townsfolk's enjoyment, Aladdin proposed joining forces with Captain Cook, leading to the creation of "Grass Happens & Dragons Flame," a combination of lawn care and performance art. Together, they toured the kingdom, turning their competition into collaboration and proving that the best business partners often come from unlikely friendships. Through their adventure, they learned that teamwork and creativity could turn challenges into successes.

Name: _____ # _____

Summer Jobs, Captain Hook and a Dragon

Characters: Narrator 1, Narrator 2, Aladdin, Cinderella, Genie, Hansel, Gretel, Rapunzel, Prince Eric, Captain Cook, Tink

Narrator 1 : Once upon a time, in a land where fairy tales intertwined, a group of cherished characters convened with a dream that shimmered in their eyes.

Narrator 2: Aladdin, with a twinkle of ambition, sparked the conversation.

Aladdin: Friends, it's time we turn our tales into success. I need cash for school clothes.

Cinderella: I'm so with you. This dress has been around for centuries. Literally. And I can't get the bird stains out. It won't make it one more year.

Belle: At least you two don't parade around looking like you're perpetually lost in Wonderland. I swear my creator and Lewis Carroll shopped at the same stores.

Narrator 1: Enter Genie. Followed by Rapunzel, Prince Eric, Hansel, and Gretel.

Narrator 2: They too wanted to earn summer cash.

Genie: How about mowing lawns? With my magical mowing app, we're destined for success!

Aladdin: Is that what you've been working on?

Genie: Behold, the 'Grass Master 3000'!" A high-tech lawn mowing app.

Hansel: Let's call our business "Grass Happens."

Rapunzel: It'll be great to get some exercise. I'm get dizzy walking in circles in my tower.

Prince Eric: There'll be no sea witches will there?

Gretel: Not a one. We'll steer clear Seaweed way.

Prince Eric: Then count me in for a land adventure.

Cinderella: The more the merrier.

Narrator: The team was off to an astounding success.

Narrator 2: Then came Captain Hook, now Captain Cook, with a dragon in tow.

Belle: What happened to the crocodile?

Captain Cook: Foiled by none other than Peter Pan. This is my new dragon breathing mowing system. We're here to mow lawns and I don't think this place is big enough for two business.

Rapunzel: If we don't act, my hopes for a Dyson are dashed. These locks can't tame themselves.

Prince Eric: It's Hook—or Cook's—circus act. That dragon is stealing our show.

Hansel: Let's have a lawn-off to settle this. See who truly reigns over the grass.

83

Summer Jobs, Captain Hook and a Dragon - page 2

Gretel: Exactly! The winner takes all the glory...and the grass.

Narrator: A challenge was thrown across the streets, accepted with a mixture of intrigue and mischief.

Narrator 2: At dawn, the competition commenced, judged by none other than Tinker Bell, a dear friend of Rapunzel.

Tink: May the best team win! Begin!

Narrator: Chaos unfolded. Captain Cook's dragon turned hedges into fireworks. His whole block was ablaze.

Narrator 2: While Genie's app glitched and transformed lawns into disco dance floors.

Prince Eric: Woah, not looking good for anyone.

Gretel: Except the spectators. Look at the crowds.

Narrator 2: The crowds were huge. People came in droves to watch the show.

Narrator : Aladdin saw an opportunity not just in lawn care, but entertainment.

Aladdin: Captain, what say we join forces? Our talents combined could redefine lawn care and entertainment.

Captain Cook: Hm... Arr, let's set this venture ablaze! What be our name?

Rapunzel: Grass Happens & Dragons Flame!

Genie: Perfect! Together, we'll mow and dazzle, spreading joy and perfectly trimmed lawns across the kingdom.

Cinderella: And I'll talk to my stepmother. She's head of FBS – the Fairy tale Broadcast System. We can do a reality TV show. Stream our work.

Narrator: And so, they did. From rivalry to unity, they discovered that collaboration not only breeds success but forges friendships and joy beyond measure.

Narrator 2: Their tale of unexpected alliances became legendary - and their reality show was number one for years to come.

All: And we all mowed happily ever after.

Teacher Page   Name: _____ # _____

WHOLE CLASS ACTIVITY Compare and Contrast - Story vs. Readers Theater

Whole class assignment after this readers theater. Have student or teacher read Version 1.0 of the story. Then work together on the compare and contrast assignment.

Characters Similarity: Both versions feature a cast from fairy tales with a modern entrepreneurial twist, including Aladdin, Cinderella, Genie, Hansel, Gretel, Rapunzel, Prince Eric, and Captain Cook (Hook). They come together with the common goal of earning money, initially through lawn care, which showcases their adaptability and teamwork.

Settings and Dialogue Differences:

- **Settings:** The story's setting emphasizes the fairy tale land with a focus on the lawn care business, including challenges from Captain Cook and his dragon. The readers theater, while similar, places more emphasis on the interactions between characters and their plans to overcome business challenges.

- **Dialogue:** The dialogue in the reader's theater script is more direct and concise, focusing on advancing the plot through spoken words. The story, on the other hand, allows for more descriptive language and inner thoughts of characters, providing a richer context.

Settings and Dialogue Similarities:

- Both versions are set in a whimsical fairy tale land where characters use modern entrepreneurship to solve their problems. The dialogue in both retains humor and cleverness, reflecting the characters' personalities and the fantastical setting.

Dialogue Enhancement through Reader's Theater: The reader's theater script enhances the story by bringing the dialogue to the forefront, making interactions more dynamic and immediate. This format allows characters' voices and personalities to shine, offering a different engagement level with the audience through performance.

Main Events Analysis:

- **Similarities:** Both the narrative and the reader's theater depict the formation of a lawn care business, challenges from Captain Cook and his dragon, a competition, and eventual collaboration between the characters for mutual benefit.

- **Differences:** The reader's theater script focuses more on dialogue and interactions, making events feel more immediate and engaging through spoken word. The narrative provides a broader description, internal thoughts, and detailed actions, offering a more comprehensive view of events.

Reader's Theater Script Main Events:

- Formation of "Grass Happens"
- Arrival of Captain Cook and his dragon, posing a challenge
- The lawn-off competition and its chaotic outcome
- Proposal of collaboration and creation of "Grass Happens & Dragons Flame"
- Narrative or Story Main Events:
- Same key events but with added descriptive details and character thoughts
- More focus on the emotional journey and development of the characters
- Exploration of themes like entrepreneurship, rivalry, and friendship

The reader's theater script brings a lively and interactive dimension to the story, emphasizing dialogue and character interaction. In contrast, the narrative form provides a richer, more nuanced exploration of the characters' inner worlds and the magical setting. Both forms offer unique experiences of the same core tale, highlighting the creativity and adaptability of fairy tale characters in modern entrepreneurial ventures.

Name: _____ # _____

Compare and Contrast - Story vs. Readers Theater

Directions: Please use complete sentences to answer the questions.

Version Title: Summer Jobs, Captain Hook and a Dragon

How are the characters in the reader's theater script similar to the characters in the story?
_____
_____
_____

How are the settings and dialogue in the reader's theater script different from those in the story?
_____
_____
_____

How are the settings and dialogue in the reader's theater script the same as those in the story?
_____
_____
_____

How does the use of dialogue in the reader's theater script enhance the story differently than the narrative form?
_____
_____
_____
_____

What are the main events in both the reader's theater script and the narrative, and how are they presented differently in each version?	
Reader's Theater Script Main Events	Narrative or Story Main Events
Similarities:	Similarities:
Differences:	Differences:

Teacher Page

Summer Jobs, Captain Hook and a Dragon

Theme: The theme of the story revolves around entrepreneurship, creativity, and collaboration. It emphasizes the value of teamwork and adaptability in overcoming challenges and finding innovative solutions.

Setting: The story takes place in a fairy-tale world, involving magical characters and elements. The setting includes common places like towns and lawns but is spiced up with fantastical elements like magic and dragons.

Character Traits

- **Cinderella**: Practical and aware of the need for change.
- **Belle**: Observant and eager for innovation.
- **Rapunzel**: Willing to contribute beyond her known traits, showing initiative.
- **Aladdin**: Entrepreneurial and proactive with ideas.
- **Prince Eric**: Supportive and light-hearted.
- **Genie**: Creative and dramatic, adds magic to the business.
- **Captain Cook**: Initially antagonistic but open to compromise and collaboration.

Main Idea: The main idea of the story is to highlight how a group of fairy-tale characters uses their unique abilities and teamwork to create and adapt a business venture, learning the importance of cooperation over competition in the process.

Problem: The problem arises when Captain Cook and his dragon threaten to eliminate the competition posed by the protagonists' lawn care business, leading to a conflict.

Solution: The solution is found when the protagonists propose a friendly competition to Captain Cook, which eventually leads to a chaotic but entertaining outcome. Recognizing the public's enjoyment of the spectacle, they decide to collaborate rather than compete, combining their efforts into a new, successful venture that blends lawn care with performance art.

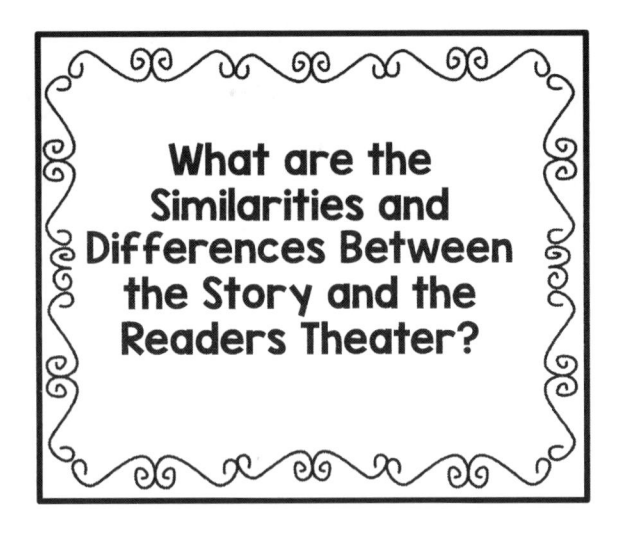

Name: _____ # _____

Summer Jobs, Captain Hook and a Dragon
Compare and Contrast - Interactive Notebook

Directions: Cut along solid lines, attach at the dashed line. Make a book by placing one shape on top of the other and attaching it to your notebook

What are the Similarities and Differences Between the Story and the Readers Theater?

Differences

Summer Jobs, Captain Hook and a Dragon

Similarities

Summer Jobs, Captain Hook and a Dragon

Name: _____ # _____

Summer Jobs, Captain Hook and a Dragon
Theme - Interactive Notebook

<u>**Directions:**</u> Cut along solid lines, glue under "Theme."

Theme

How does the theme of teamwork and collaboration contribute to the success and happiness of the characters in the story "Summer Jobs, Captain Hook and a Dragon"?

Summer Jobs, Captain Hook and a Dragon

89

Name: _____ # _____

**Summer Jobs, Captain Hook and a Dragon
Theme - Interactive Notebook**

Directions: Cut along solid lines, attach at the dashed line. Make a book, placing one shape on top of the other and attaching the booklet to your notebook.

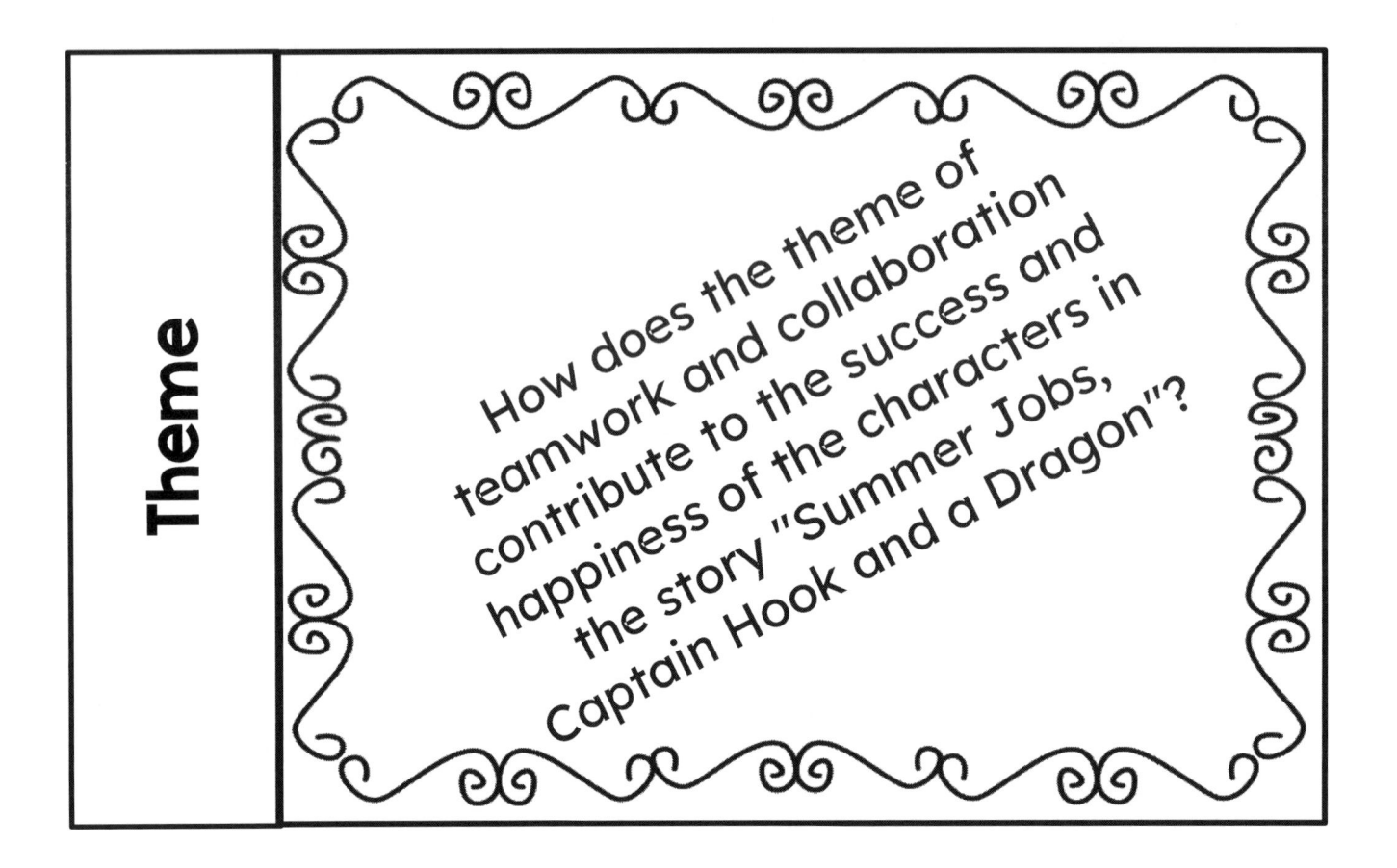

Theme

How does the theme of teamwork and collaboration contribute to the success and happiness of the characters in the story "Summer Jobs, Captain Hook and a Dragon"?

In "Summer Jobs, Captain Hook and a Dragon," teamwork and collaboration are essential as the characters unite their unique abilities to form a successful lawn care business and later partner with their rival, Captain Cook, enhancing their success and spreading joy throughout the kingdom. This cooperative spirit not only leads to their venture's triumph but also fosters happiness and unexpected friendships, proving the power of working together.

Character Traits

Character traits are qualities or characteristics that describe what a person is like. It's how someone behaves and thinks.

Choose two characters and describe their character traits

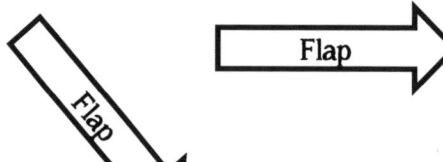

Flap

Flap

Character Traits
Summer Jobs, Captain Hook and a Dragon

Actions: _____
_____
_____
_____

Thoughts: _____
_____
_____
_____

Defining Quote: _____
_____
_____
_____

Actions _____
_____
_____
_____

Thoughts: _____
_____
_____

Defining Quote: _____
_____
_____
_____

Box 2

Directions: Cut along the outside of the shapes. Glue under the flaps. Glue Box 2 into your notebook. Glue Box one under flap on top and place on top of Box 2. Glue "Character Traits" under flap to create a cover for the pages on top.

91

Name: _____ # _____

Making Inferences RL.1 **Summer Jobs, Captain Hook and a Dragon**

Directions: Cut along the outside of the shapes. Glue into your notebook. Glue under the flap and attach to write under the flap. Choose a quote from the story. Write it under the "What Was Said" flap. Write what you think the quote means, or implies, under the "What It Implies" flap.

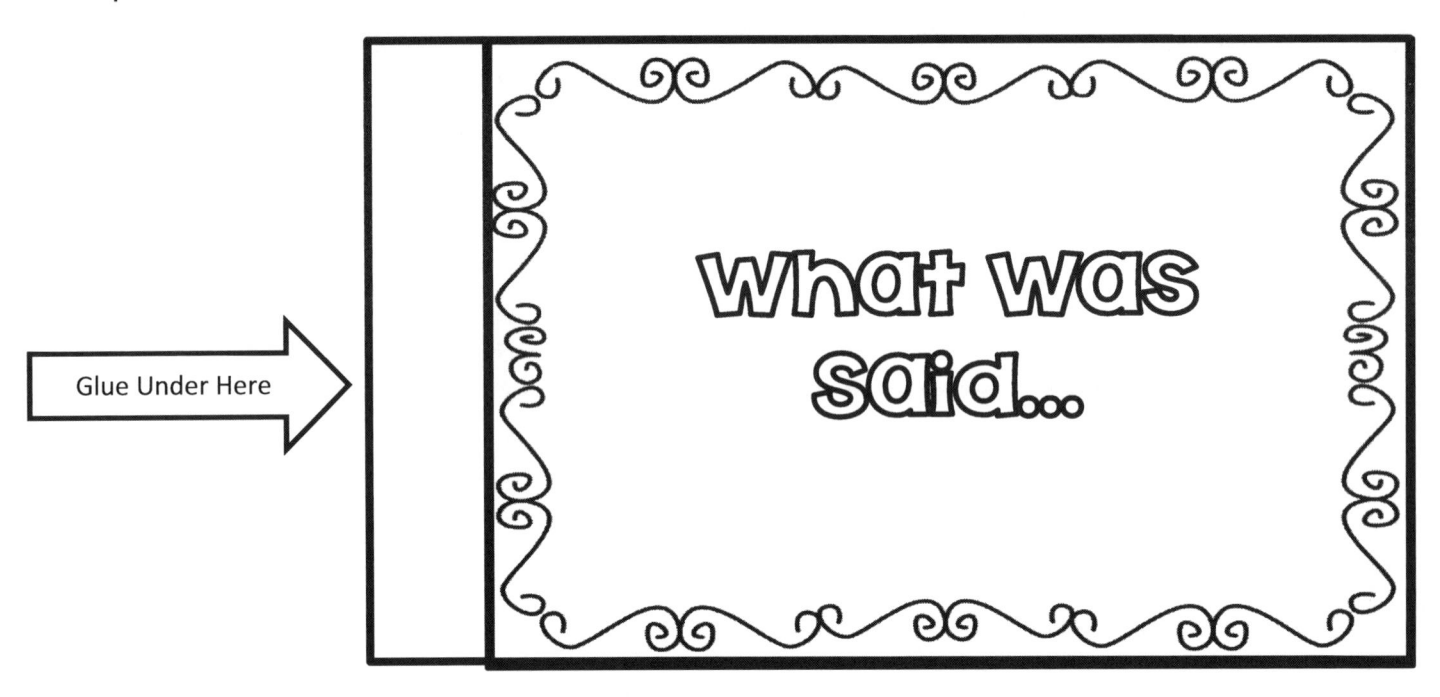

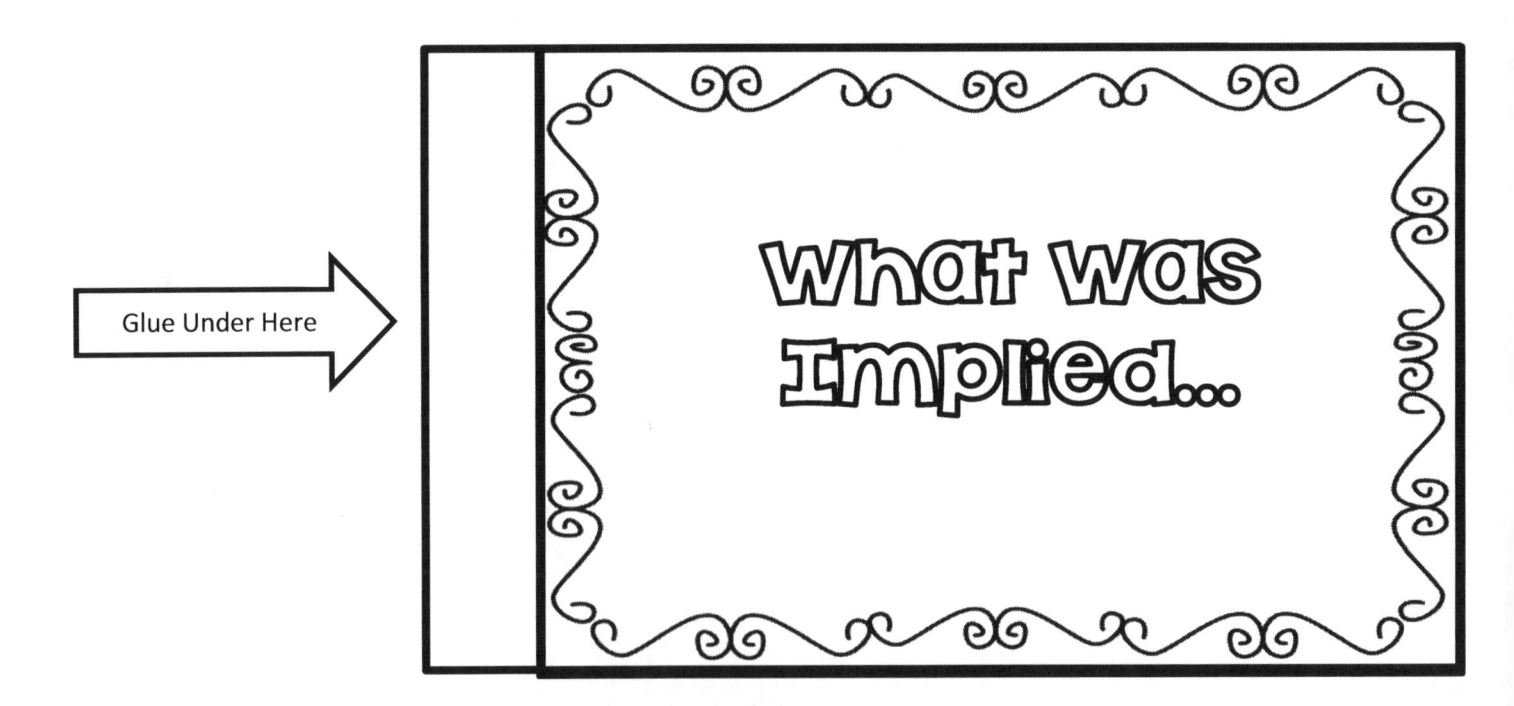

Glue Under Here →

What was said...

Glue Under Here →

What was Implied...

Inference: An inference is a conclusion drawn from evidence from your reading, your thoughts and what you know about life and events.

92

Name: _____ # _____

Making Inferences RL 1

Summer Jobs, Captain Hook and a Dragon

Directions: Cut on the solid lines. Fold on the dotted lines. Glue or tape the center to your notebook. Answer the questions under the flaps.

Inference: An inference is a conclusion drawn from evidence in your reading, your thoughts and what you know about life and events.

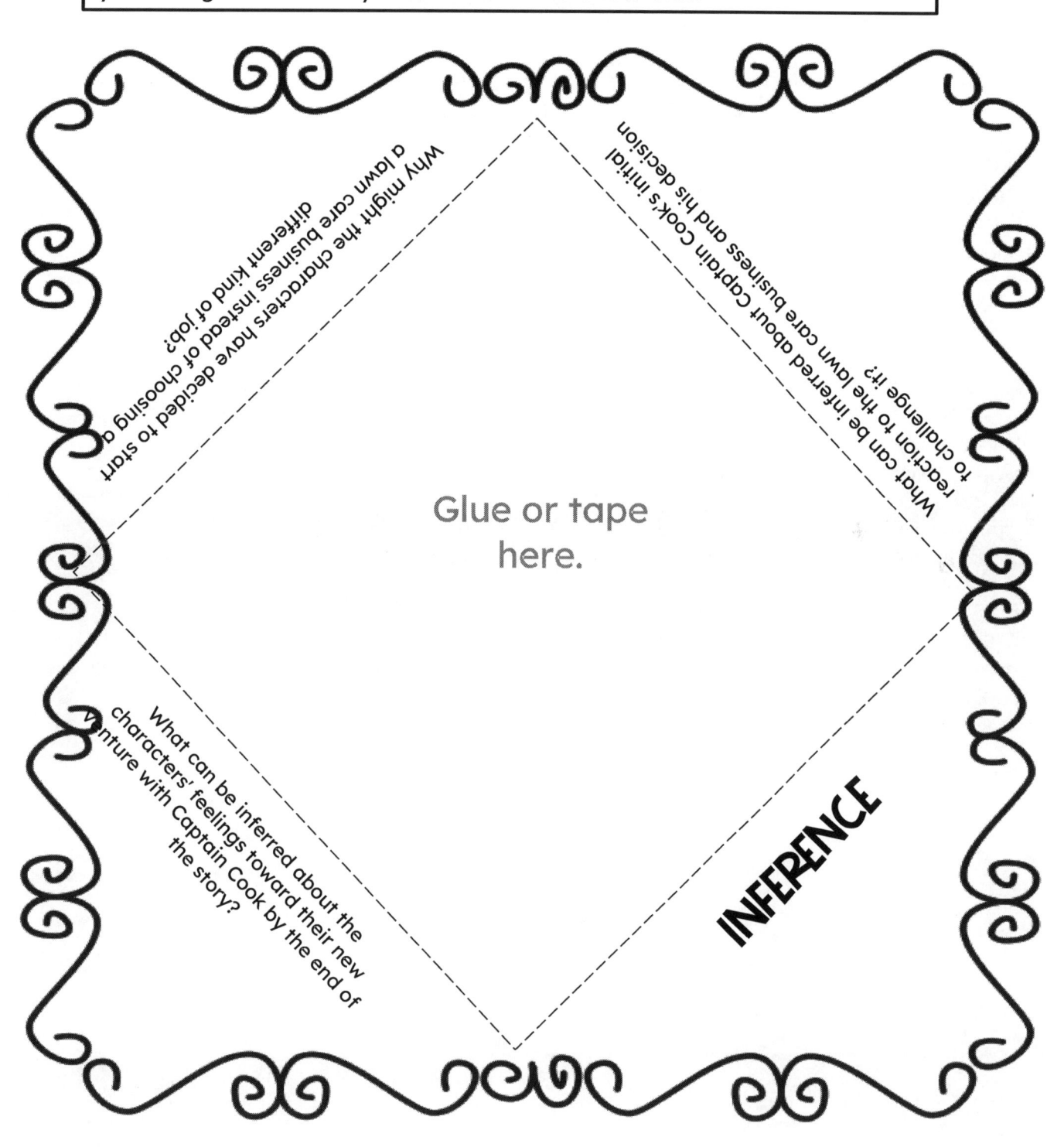

- Why might the characters have decided to start a lawn care business instead of choosing a different kind of job?
- What can be inferred about the lawn care business and Captain Cook's initial reaction to challenge it?
- What can be inferred about the characters' feelings toward their new venture with Captain Cook by the end of the story?

Glue or tape here.

INFERENCE

93

Teacher Page

Name: _____ # _____

Making Inferences RL 1

Summer Jobs, Captain Hook and a Dragon

Directions: Cut on the solid lines. Fold on the dotted lines. Glue or tape the center to your notebook. Answer the questions under the flaps.

> **Inference:** An inference is a conclusion drawn from evidence in your reading, your thoughts and what you know about life and events.

1. **Question:** Why might the characters have decided to start a lawn care business instead of choosing a different kind of job?

The characters likely chose to start a lawn care business because they saw an opportunity to use their unique abilities, like Genie's magic, in a practical way to meet a need in their community, demonstrating creativity and resourcefulness in solving their problem of needing money for school clothes.

2. **Question:** What can be inferred about Captain Cook's initial reaction to the lawn care business and his decision to challenge it?

Captain Cook's initial reaction to challenge the lawn care business suggests he felt threatened by the competition and wanted to assert his dominance. However, his eventual decision to join forces implies he recognized the value of collaboration over rivalry, learning that working together could lead to mutual benefits.

3. **Question:** How does the story imply that the townsfolk feel about the transformation of lawn care into a performance art?

The story implies that the townsfolk enjoy and appreciate the transformation of lawn care into performance art, as it not only beautifies their community but also provides entertainment, indicating that innovative and joyful approaches to everyday tasks are valued and celebrated by the community.

INFERENCE

Name: _____ # _____

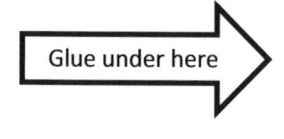

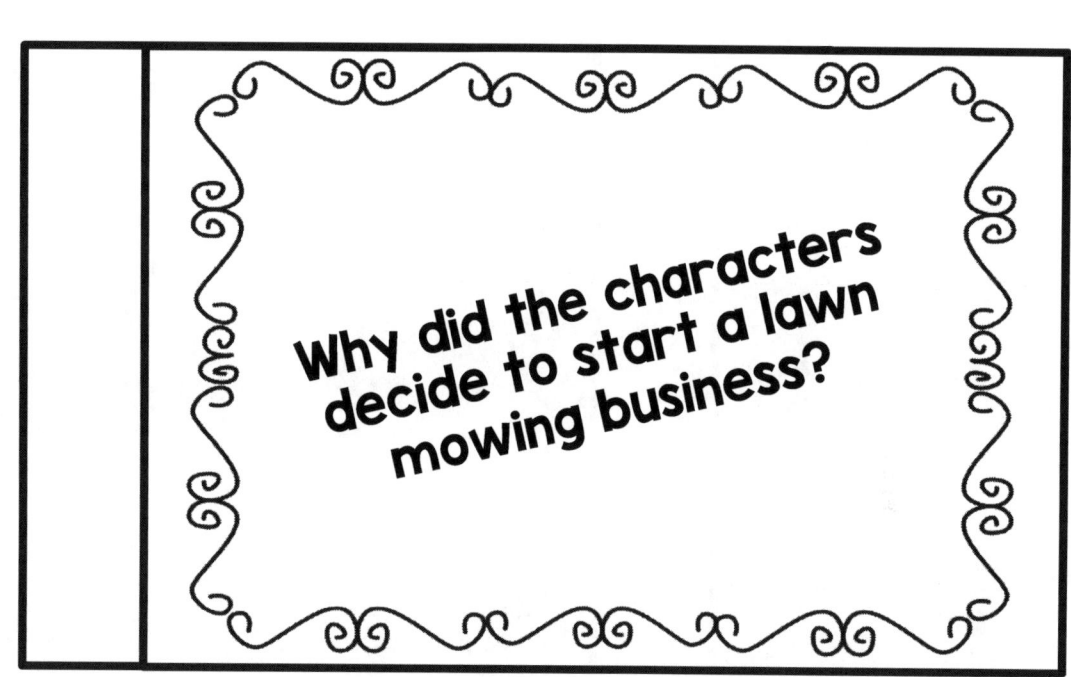

Key Ideas and Details RL.I: Cite textual evidence to support analysis of text, both inferential and explicit.

Directions: Cut along the outside of the shapes. Glue into your notebook. Glue under the flap and attach to write under the flap. Answer the question under the flap.

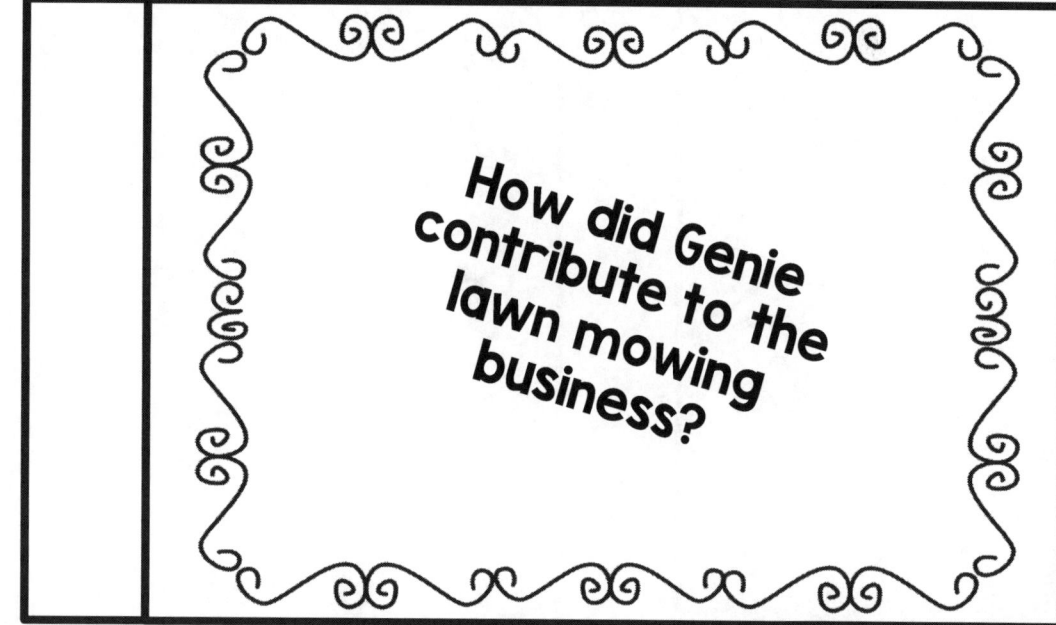

Summer Jobs, Captain Hook, and a Dragon

Glue under here →

Why did the characters decide to start a lawn mowing business?

Glue under here →

How did Genie contribute to the lawn mowing business?

95

Name: _____ # _____

Key Ideas and Details RL.1: Cite textual evidence to support analysis of text, both inferential and explicit.

Directions: Cut along the outside of the shapes. Glue into your notebook. Glue under the flap and attach to write under the flap. Answer the question under the flap.

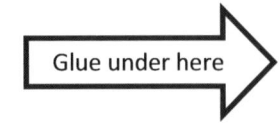

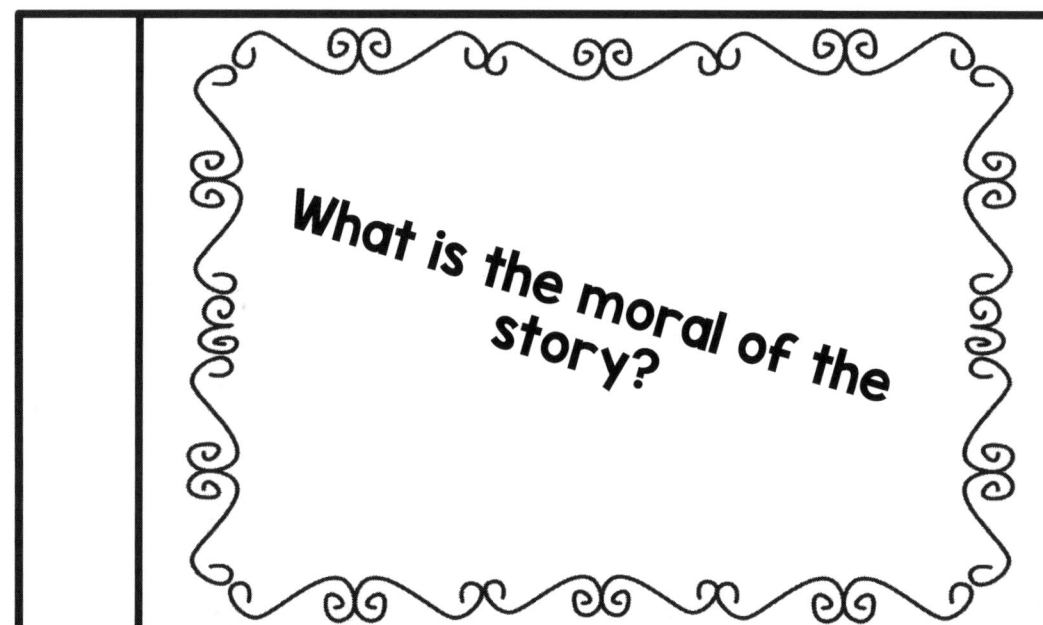

Summer Jobs, Captain Hook, and a Dragon

Glue under here →

What was Captain Hook's response to the lawn mowing business, and how was the conflict resolved?

Glue under here →

What is the moral of the story?

96

Teacher Page

Summer Jobs, Captain Hook and a Dragon

Key Ideas and Details RL.1: Cite textual evidence to support analysis of text, both inferential and explicit.

Question 1: Why did the characters decide to start a lawn mowing business?

Answer Guidance: The text explicitly states that the characters wanted to earn money for school clothes for the next year. Aladdin introduced the idea of mowing lawns as a unique business opportunity, and the others agreed, indicating their collective need to earn money and their interest in pursuing an entrepreneurial venture together.

Question 2: How did Genie contribute to the lawn mowing business?

Answer Guidance: The Genie contributed by using his magic to create the "Grass Master 3000," a lawn mower designed to enhance their business. This shows his willingness to support the venture with his unique abilities, even though the actual performance of the mower turned the grass into a disco floor instead of cutting it.

Question 3: What was Captain Hook's response to the lawn mowing business, and how was the conflict resolved?

Answer Guidance: Captain Hook, reborn as Captain Cook, and his dragon threatened to take over the lawn market, posing a challenge to the protagonists' business. The conflict was resolved when Hansel and Gretel proposed a lawn-off competition. Although the competition did not go as planned, it ended with Aladdin offering a partnership to Captain Cook, which he accepted, leading to the merging of their ventures into "Grass Happens & Dragon Trims."

Question 4: What is the moral of the story?

Answer Guidance: The moral of the story is that collaboration and teamwork can lead to success, joy, and friendship, even among unlikely allies. Despite initial competition and challenges, the characters discovered that working together not only allowed them to achieve their goals but also brought entertainment and happiness to their community, proving that unity can create greater outcomes than rivalry.

Name: _____ # _____

Key Ideas and Detail RL.2 - Theme Development

Summer Jobs, Captain Hook and a Dragon

Theme The Message. A theme is the moral or lesson of a story – it is the underlying meaning. **Analyze how the theme is developed throughout the story.**

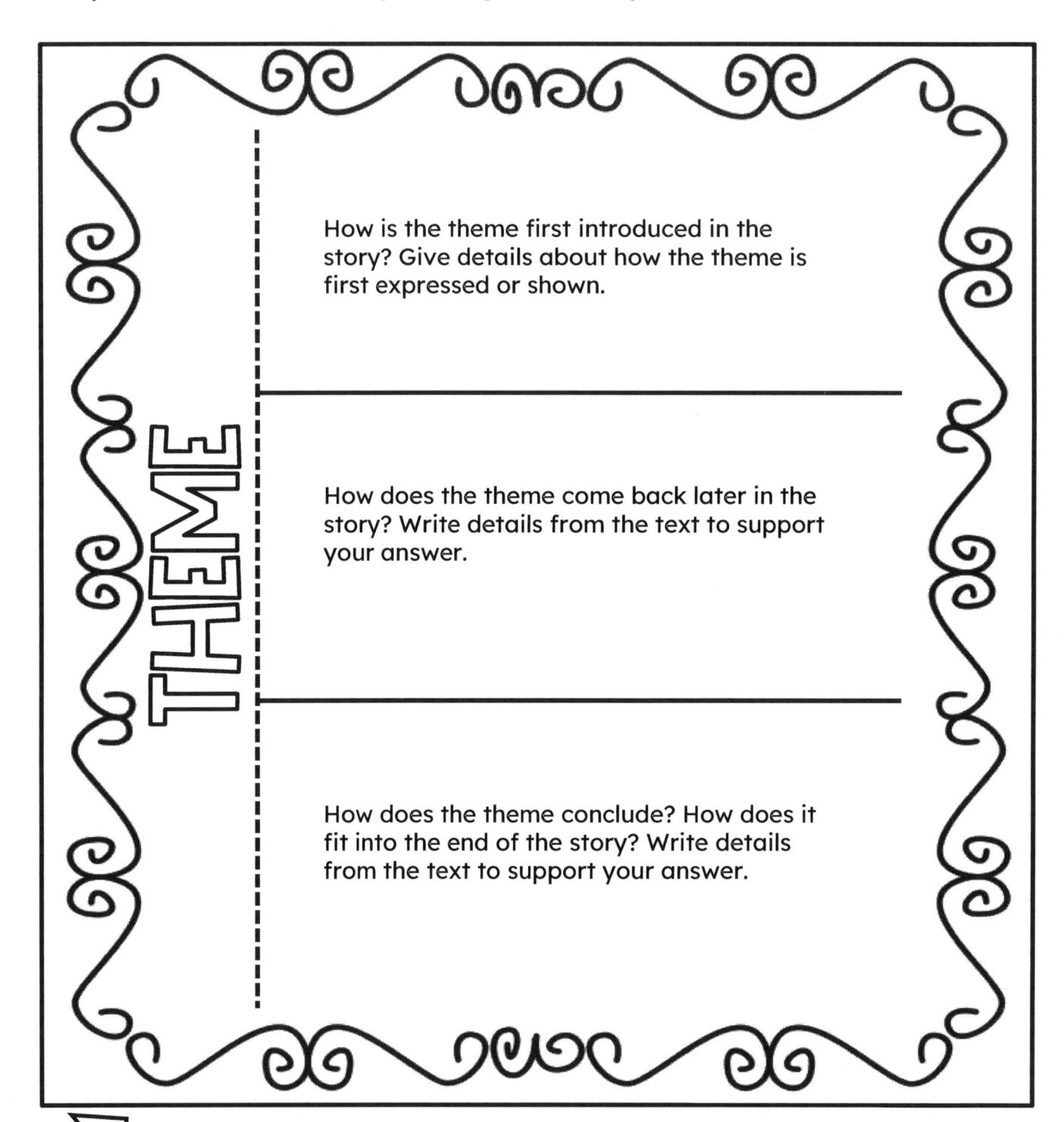

THEME

How is the theme first introduced in the story? Give details about how the theme is first expressed or shown.

_____

How does the theme come back later in the story? Write details from the text to support your answer.

_____

How does the theme conclude? How does it fit into the end of the story? Write details from the text to support your answer.

Glue under here

Directions: Cut along the solid lines. Fold along the dotted lines. Write your answer under the flaps.

Teacher Page   Name: _____ # _____

Key Ideas and Detail RL.2 - Theme Development

Summer Jobs, Captain Hook and a Dragon

Theme The Message. A theme is the moral or lesson of a story – it is the underlying meaning. Analyze how the theme is developed throughout the story.

THEME

The theme of working together to solve problems and achieve goals pops up at the beginning when the fairytale land folks decide they need money for school clothes. They all think their old clothes are boring and want something new. So, Aladdin says, "Let's mow lawns," and everyone is like, "Yeah, cool idea!" This shows they're all in to try new stuff together and help each other out.

Later in the story, when Captain Cook and his dragon try to mess up their lawn business, the theme of teamwork shines again. Hansel and Gretel come up with the idea of a lawn-off challenge. But, when things go wrong, instead of fighting or giving up, they decide to work with Captain Cook. Aladdin even offers to team up with him, showing how working together can turn enemies into friends.

In the end, everyone joins forces and creates "Grass Happens & Dragon Trims," making their business even better and more fun. They turn lawn care into something exciting for the whole kingdom, showing that when people work together, they can make something amazing that brings joy to everyone. It wraps up the story nicely, proving that teamwork not only solves problems but also creates happiness and new friendships.

Directions: Cut along the solid lines. Fold along the dotted lines. Write your answer under the flaps.

Name: _____ # _____

Key Ideas and Detail RL.2 - Sequence of Events

Directions: Cut along the solid lines. Fold along the dotted lines. Write your answer under the flaps.

Summer Jobs, Captain Hook and a Dragon

Summer Jobs, Captain Hook and a Dragon

In the Beginning,

Then,

Lastly,

Glue under here

100

Name: _____ # _____

Key Ideas and Detail RL.6 - Point of View
Analyzing the Author's Attitude

Directions: Cut along the solid lines. Fold along the dotted lines. Write your answer under the flaps.

Analyze how the writer's attitude influences the beliefs of the characters.

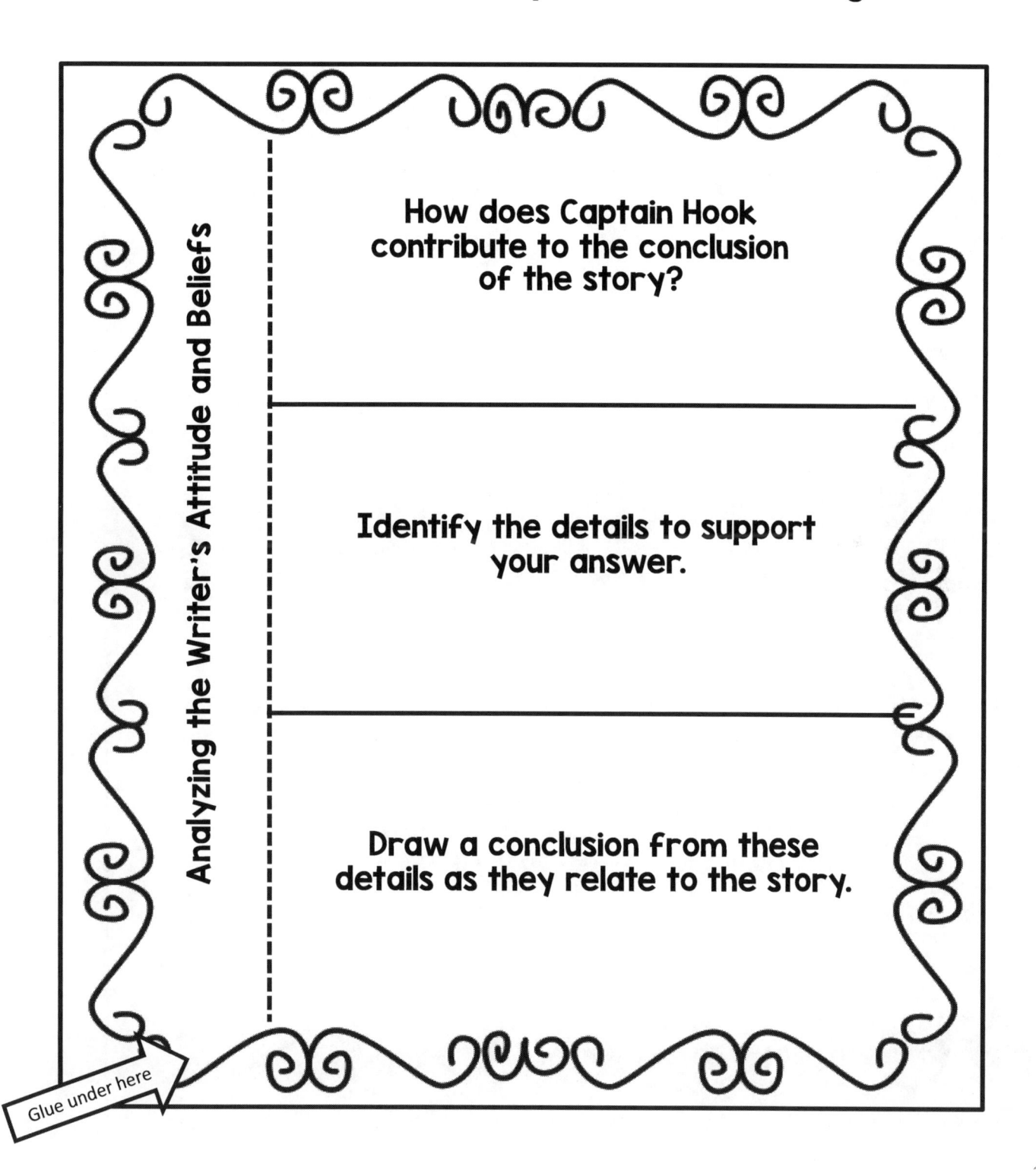

Summer Jobs, Captain Hook and a Dragon

Analyzing the Writer's Attitude and Beliefs

How does Captain Hook contribute to the conclusion of the story?

Identify the details to support your answer.

Draw a conclusion from these details as they relate to the story.

Glue under here

101

Teacher Page   Name: _____ # _____

Key Ideas and Detail RL.6 - Point of View
Analyzing the Author's Attitude

Directions: Cut along the solid lines. Fold along the dotted lines. Write your answer under the flaps.

Analyze how the writer's attitude influences the beliefs of the characters.

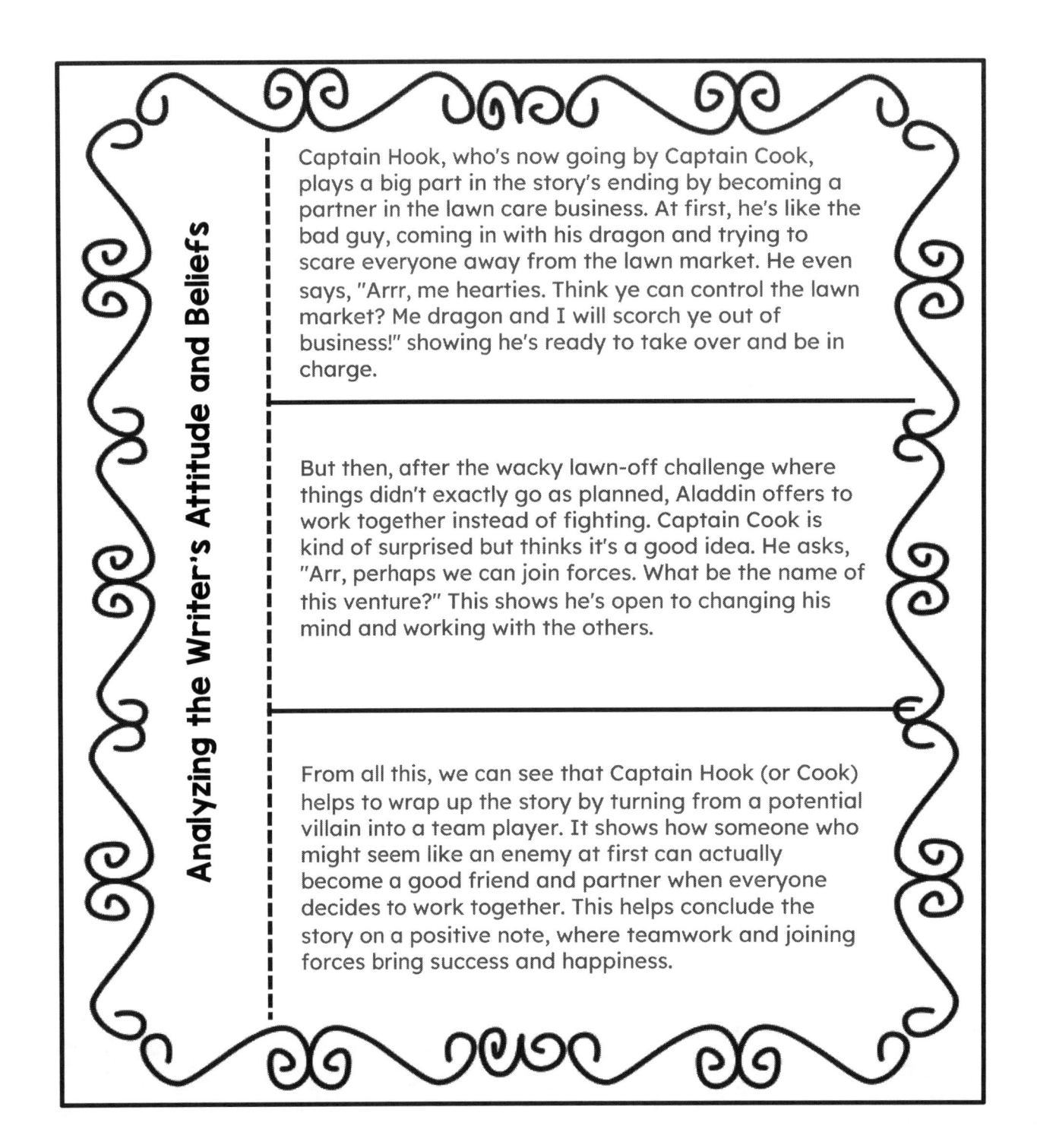

Summer Jobs, Captain Hook and a Dragon

Analyzing the Writer's Attitude and Beliefs

Captain Hook, who's now going by Captain Cook, plays a big part in the story's ending by becoming a partner in the lawn care business. At first, he's like the bad guy, coming in with his dragon and trying to scare everyone away from the lawn market. He even says, "Arrr, me hearties. Think ye can control the lawn market? Me dragon and I will scorch ye out of business!" showing he's ready to take over and be in charge.

But then, after the wacky lawn-off challenge where things didn't exactly go as planned, Aladdin offers to work together instead of fighting. Captain Cook is kind of surprised but thinks it's a good idea. He asks, "Arr, perhaps we can join forces. What be the name of this venture?" This shows he's open to changing his mind and working with the others.

From all this, we can see that Captain Hook (or Cook) helps to wrap up the story by turning from a potential villain into a team player. It shows how someone who might seem like an enemy at first can actually become a good friend and partner when everyone decides to work together. This helps conclude the story on a positive note, where teamwork and joining forces bring success and happiness.

The County Fair

The County Fair

Once upon a time, in a land where fairy tales and reality shows intersect, there was a county fair like no other, celebrated for its ability to draw characters from fairy tales near and far. This year, the fair's highlight was the "Fairy Tale Mash-Up," a competition designed to test wit, courage, and the ability to withstand reality TV level drama.

The three little pigs, architects of notoriety, had teamed up with Snow White, the fairest of them all, who had grown quite adept at managing diverse personalities, thanks to her time with the seven dwarfs. They were set to face their long-time rival, the Big Bad Wolf, who, rumor had it, had been taking charisma lessons from Puss in Boots.

"Diversifying my skill set," smirked the Wolf, flashing a grin that was part charm and part menace.

Their challenge was to design and construct the most enchanting and structurally sound booth at the fair. The twist? They had to incorporate elements from each of their stories and to highlight crops from their region of origin. This was a county fair after all.

The judges, a panel comprising of Fairy Godmother, the Cheshire Cat, and an unusually serious Humpty Dumpty, were looking for creativity, practicality, and a dash of magic.

"I propose a brick booth, sturdy and wolf-proof," declared the eldest pig, always the practical one.

"With an apple-themed snack bar!" chimed in Snow White, ever the optimist, ignoring the collective shudder from her team at the mention of apples. "They are crops from our region."

"Just not the poison kind," snapped Grumpy.

"And a mirror selfie station!" added Dopey, twirling around and nearly knocking over a stack of blueprints.

"Let's not forget about security," Grumpy muttered, eyeing the Big Bad Wolf's booth with suspicion. "I wouldn't put it past that furball to try something sneaky."

The construction of the booth was a cacophony of hammers, magic, and the occasional argument over aesthetic choices. The Wolf, on the other paw, was taking a different approach. His booth was a spectacle of high-tech gimmicks and flashy presentations, designed to charm the socks off anyone within a hundred-foot radius.

"Who needs bricks when you have holograms?" the Wolf boasted, as his booth displayed a dazzling light show.

The day of the judging arrived, and the fairgrounds were buzzing with excitement. The three pigs and Snow White's booth was a marvel of and charm, with brick walls adorned with apple motifs and a bustling snack bar.

The County Fair - page 2

Dopey manned the selfie station, which had become an instant hit, while Doc offered guided tours, explaining the engineering marvels behind their construction and all the different kinds of apples that grow in their particular part of the woods.

Meanwhile, the Wolf's booth, while initially impressive, began to show its flaws. The holograms flickered and faded, and the high-tech gadgets proved more style than substance. As for crops from his region – he'd failed to include anything but a couple of mushrooms and some straw.

When it came time for the verdict, the judges were unanimous. The three pigs, Snow White, and the dwarfs were declared the winners, their booth a testament to teamwork, durability, and genuine enchantment.

"Looks like substance wins over style," laughed Doc, as they were handed the trophy.

The Wolf, defeated but not discouraged, approached the winners. "I suppose there's something to be said for the classics. Would you consider a joint venture next year? I've got some ideas that, with your touch, could really blow everyone away—metaphorically speaking, of course."

The pigs exchanged glances, Snow White smiled warmly, and even Grumpy seemed to consider the proposition.

"Let's talk," said the eldest pig, extending a hand to the Wolf. "After all, every story can benefit from a little twist."

"Until next year then," the Wolf bowed.

"Until then," smiled Snow White as Grumpy handed the Wolf a basket of apples. An uncharacteristically kind gesture from the grumpiest of them all.

Or was it?

Name: _____ # _____

The County Fair - V.I

1. What was the main event at the county fair?
   a. A pie-eating contest
   b. The "Fairy Tale Mash-Up" competition
   c. A magic show
   d. A jousting tournament

2. Who teamed up with the three little pigs for the competition?
   a. Cinderella
   b. The Mad Hatter
   c. Snow White
   d. Peter Pan

3. What unique element did the three pigs and Snow White's booth have?
   a. A hologram display
   b. A brick construction with apple motifs
   c. A pumpkin carriage
   d. A spinning wheel

4. Who were the judges of the competition?
   a. Merlin, King Arthur, and Robin Hood
   b. Aladdin, Jasmine, and the Genie
   c. The Witch, the Huntsman, and the Mirror
   d. The Fairy Godmother, the Cheshire Cat, and Humpty Dumpty

5. What was the main flaw in the Big Bad Wolf's booth?
   a. It was made of straw.
   b. It had no roof.
   c. The holograms flickered and faded.
   d. It was too small.

6. What did the Big Bad Wolf propose at the end of the story?
   a. A joint venture for the next year
   b. A rematch at next year's fair
   c. A solo venture to redeem himself
   d. Leaving the county fair for good

7. 7. Summarize the story in five to six sentences.

_____
_____
_____
_____
_____
_____

Teacher Page   Name: _____ # _____

The County Fair - V.I

1. What was the main event at the county fair?
    a. A pie-eating contest
    b. The "Fairy Tale Mash-Up" competition
    c. A magic show
    d. A jousting tournament

2. Who teamed up with the three little pigs for the competition?
    a. Cinderella
    b. The Mad Hatter
    c. Snow White
    d. Peter Pan

3. What unique element did the three pigs and Snow White's booth have?
    a. A hologram display
    b. A brick construction with apple motifs
    c. A pumpkin carriage
    d. A spinning wheel

4. Who were the judges of the competition?
    a. Merlin, King Arthur, and Robin Hood
    b. Aladdin, Jasmine, and the Genie
    c. The Witch, the Huntsman, and the Mirror
    d. The Fairy Godmother, the Cheshire Cat, and Humpty Dumpty

5. What was the main flaw in the Big Bad Wolf's booth?
    a. It was made of straw.
    b. It had no roof.
    c. The holograms flickered and faded.
    d. It was too small.

6. What did the Big Bad Wolf propose at the end of the story?
    a. A joint venture for the next year
    b. A rematch at next year's fair
    c. A solo venture to redeem himself
    d. Leaving the county fair for good

7. 7. Summarize the story in five to six sentences.

_____
_____
_____
_____
_____
_____

Name: _____ # _____

The County Fair

Once upon a time there was a county fair. It wasn't a normal county fair. It was in the land of fairy tales. Well, the land of fairy tales and reality shows. This year there was a contest at the fair. It was called "Fairy Tale Mash-Up."

The three little pig had teamed up with Snow White. Who were they were up against? None other than the Big Bad Wolf. Who had been taking lessons on how to be nice from Puss-in-Boots.

"Blowing up my skill set," smirked the Wolf. He flashed a grin that looked charming. But there was something else too. Something so very un-charming.

Their task was to build the most enchanting booth at the fair. The twist? They had to include things from each of their stories. They also had to add crops from their settings. This was a county fair after all.

The judges were the Fairy Godmother, the Cheshire Cat, and a grumpy Humpty Dumpty. The judges were looking for creativity, soundness, and a dash of magic.

"I propose a brick booth. It is wolf-proof," declared the eldest pig. "It'll also keep away the stray witch.

"With an apple-themed snack bar!" Snow White said. "They are crops from our region."

"Just not the poison kind," snapped Grumpy.

"And a mirror selfie station!" added Dopey. He spun around. He nearly knocked over a stack of blueprints.

"Let's not forget about security," Grumpy muttered. He eyed the Big Bad Wolf's booth. "I wouldn't put it past that furball to try something on us."

Their booths went up in no time.

The Wolf, on the other paw, went a different way. His booth was a spectacle of high-tech gimmicks and flashy presentations, designed to charm the socks off anyone within a hundred-foot radius.

"Who needs bricks when you have holograms?" The Wolf pushed a button. His booth lit up.

The day of the judging came. The fairgrounds were buzzing. The three pigs and Snow White's booth was charming. The brick walls had apples painted on them. The snack bar was tasty. It was also busy. Dopey was at the selfie station. The selfies were a hit. Doc gave tours. He also showed off the apples. There were many kinds. None were poison.

The County Fair - page 2

The Wolf's booth was cool at first. Then – not so much. The holograms flickered and faded. The high-tech gadgets fizzled. As for his crops – he only had some mushrooms and old logs.

The three pigs, Snow White, and the dwarfs won easily. Their booth showed teamwork and flair.

The Wolf lost. But he was not discouraged. He walked up to the winners. "I guess there's something to be said for the classics. Would you consider doing a booth together next year? I've got some ideas. With your touch, could really blow everyone away. Metaphorically speaking, of course."

"We already did," Grumpy smirked. Snow White elbowed him.

"Let's talk," said the eldest pig. He shook the Wolf's hand. "After all, every story can benefit from a little twist."

"Until next year then," the Wolf bowed.

"Until then," smiled Snow White as Grumpy handed the Wolf a basket of apples. An uncharacteristically kind gesture from the grumpiest of them all.

Or was it?

Name: _____ # _____

The County Fair - V.2

1. Where was the county fair?
    a. In the land of fairy tales and reality shows
    b. In a big city
    c. On a farm
    d. In a forest

2. Who did the three little pigs team up with?
    a. Cinderella
    b. Snow White
    c. The Big Bad Wolf
    d. Puss in Boots

3. What did the Wolf use in his booth instead of bricks?
    a. Magic spells
    b. Straw
    c. Wood
    d. Holograms

4. Who were the judges of the contest?
    a. Three Blind Mice
    b. The Fairy Godmother, the Cheshire Cat, and Humpty Dumpty
    c. Goldilocks and the Three Bears
    d. Hansel and Gretel

5. What problem did the Wolf's booth have?
    a. It was too small.
    b. The holograms stopped working.
    c. It caught fire.
    d. It was blown away.

6. What did the Wolf propose at the end of the story?
    a. To leave the fair forever
    b. To eat everyone
    c. To work together next year
    d. To build a bigger booth alone

7. Summarize the story in five to six sentences.

Teacher Page

Name: _____ # _____

The County Fair - V.2

1. Where was the county fair?
    a. In the land of fairy tales and reality shows
    b. In a big city
    c. On a farm
    d. In a forest

2. Who did the three little pigs team up with?
    a. Cinderella
    b. Snow White
    c. The Big Bad Wolf
    d. Puss in Boots

3. What did the Wolf use in his booth instead of bricks?
    a. Magic spells
    b. Straw
    c. Wood
    d. Holograms

4. Who were the judges of the contest?
    a. Three Blind Mice
    b. The Fairy Godmother, the Cheshire Cat, and Humpty Dumpty
    c. Goldilocks and the Three Bears
    d. Hansel and Gretel

5. What problem did the Wolf's booth have?
    a. It was too small.
    b. The holograms stopped working.
    c. It caught fire.
    d. It was blown away.

6. What did the Wolf propose at the end of the story?
    a. To leave the fair forever
    b. To eat everyone
    c. To work together next year
    d. To build a bigger booth alone

7. Summarize the story in five to six sentences.

_____
_____
_____
_____
_____
_____

Name: _____ # _____

The County Fair - Figurative Language

Characters: Narrator 1, Narrator 2, Eldest Pig, Snow White, Grumpy, Big Bad Wolf, Dopey, Youngest Pig, Judge

Narrator 1: Once upon a time, in a land where fairy tales and reality shows intersected, a county fair like no other drew characters from fables near and far.

Narrator 2: This year's highlight? The "Fairy Tale Mash-Up," a competition designed to test wit, courage, and the ability to withstand reality TV level drama.

Eldest Pig: We, the architects of notoriety, alongside Snow White, the fairest and most adept at managing diverse personalities, propose a brick booth, sturdy and wolf-proof.

Snow White: And let's add an apple-themed snack bar! A nod to the crops from our region.

Grumpy: Just not the poison kind.

Narrator: Despite a collective shudder from her team at the mention of apples, Snow White's optimism remained undimmed.

Narrator 2: Meanwhile, the Big Bad Wolf, rumored to have been taking charisma lessons from Puss in Boots, smirks at his rivals.

Big Bad Wolf: Diversifying my skill set. Who needs bricks when you have holograms?

Narrator 1: The challenge? To design and construct the most enchanting and structurally sound booth, incorporating elements from each of their stories.

Narrator 2: The judges, comprising Fairy Godmother, the Cheshire Cat, and an unusually serious Humpty Dumpty, awaited a creation crammed with creativity, practicality, and a dash of magic.

Grumpy: And let's not forget about security.

Dopey: And a mirror selfie station! Mirror, mirror on the wall..

Youngest Pig: Don't eat the apples or you'll fall.

Grumpy: We're washing the apples. Come on. We have a lot of work to do.

Narrator 1: As construction commences, the fairground becomes a cacophony of hammers, magic, and debates over aesthetics.

Narrator 2: The Wolf, opting for a spectacle of high-tech gimmicks, boasts about the superiority of holograms over traditional brick.

Wolf: My booth will charm the socks off anyone within a hundred-foot radius.

Narrator 1: Judgment day arrives, and the fairgrounds buzz with excitement. The booth crafted by the three pigs and Snow White is a marvel of charm, featuring brick walls adorned with apple motifs and a bustling snack bar.

Narrator 2: Meanwhile, the Wolf's initially impressive booth begins to show its flaws, with flickering holograms and a lack of substance.

Name: _____ # _____

The County Fair - Figurative Language

Judge: We declare the three pigs, Snow White, and the dwarfs the winners. Their booth stands as a testament to teamwork, durability, and genuine enchantment.

Doc: Looks like substance wins over style.

Narrator: In a twist of fate, the defeated Wolf approaches the winners, proposing a joint venture for the next year, suggesting that even the classics can benefit from a little twist.

Wolf: I've got ideas that, with your touch, could really blow everyone away—metaphorically speaking, of course.

Eldest Pig: Let's talk. After all, every story can benefit from a little twist.

Snow White: Until next year then.

Narrator: As Grumpy hands the Wolf a basket of apples, an uncharacteristically kind gesture hints at a new narrative, weaving a tale of rivalry turned camaraderie, and the timeless lesson that substance—and a touch of cooperation—truly wins over style.

Narrator 2: Or does it?

Name: _____ # _____

Key Ideas and Detail RL.2 - Theme Development

THEME

How is the theme first introduced in the story? Give details about how the theme is first expressed or shown.

How does the theme come back later in the story? Write details from the text to support your answer.

How does the theme conclude? How does it fit into the end of the story? Write details from the text to support your answer.

Theme The Message. A theme is the moral or lesson of a story – it is the underlying meaning. Analyze how the theme is developed throughout the story.

Flap

Glue Top Here

1

2

Directions: Box 2: Cut shapes along the solid lines. Glue shape two into your notebook. Box 1: Cut along the solid lines. Fold along the dotted lines. Write your answer under the flaps.

115

Teacher Page   Name: _____ # _____

Key Ideas and Detail RL.2 - Theme Development

THEME

Theme The Message. A theme is the moral or lesson of a story – it is the underlying meaning. **Analyze how the theme is developed throughout the story.**

1. **How is the theme first introduced in the story?** The theme of working together and combining old ways with new ideas starts at the beginning, in a unique county fair. This isn't just any fair; it's a special one where fairy tale characters come together to show off their skills in a "Fairy Tale Mash-Up" competition. This setup introduces us to a place where teamwork and innovation are key, as seen with the three little pigs and Snow White planning to build a booth that's both sturdy and welcoming, using elements from their stories.

2. **How does the theme come back later in the story?** As the story moves forward, the theme of collaboration and blending tradition with innovation is shown through the building of the booth. The team decides to use bricks (traditional and sturdy) for their booth and add modern touches like an apple-themed snack bar and a mirror selfie station. This mix shows that they value both safety and fun, proving that working together and using a bit of old and new can create something wonderful. Meanwhile, the Big Bad Wolf's approach, focusing mainly on new technology, doesn't work out as well, highlighting the importance of balance between old and new.

3. **How does the theme conclude? How does it fit into the end of the story?** The theme wraps up with the victory of the three little pigs and Snow White at the competition. Their success isn't just because they built something strong, but also because they made it inviting and interesting for everyone. This victory shows that their approach of combining reliable methods with innovative ideas was the best. In the end, when the Wolf asks to team up for next year's fair, it suggests that even he has learned the value of mixing different strengths and working together. This ending fits perfectly with the theme, showing that teamwork and embracing both traditional and new ideas lead to success.

Directions: Box 2: Cut shapes along the solid lines. Glue shape two into your notebook. Box 1: Cut along the solid lines. Fold along the dotted lines. Write your answer under the flaps.

116

Name: _____ # _____

Story Events

Directions: Explain how each of the story events unfolds.

Setting Introduction: _____
_____
_____

Event Announcement: _____
_____
_____

Character Introduction and Team Formation: _____
_____
_____
_____
_____

Competition Criteria Revealed: _____
_____
_____
_____

Team Strategy and Construction: _____
_____
_____
_____

Rival's Approach: _____
_____
_____

The Competition: _____
_____
_____

Judgment Day: _____
_____
_____

Resolution: _____
_____
_____
_____

Teacher Page

Setting Introduction: Once upon a time, in a land where fairy tales and reality shows intersected, a unique county fair known for drawing characters from fables far and wide is introduced. The setting is a magical place where fairy tale elements blend with the competitive spirit of reality TV shows.

Event Announcement: The fair's highlight this year is the "Fairy Tale Mash-Up," a competition designed to test wit, courage, and reality TV-level drama, focusing on designing and constructing enchanting and structurally sound booths that incorporate elements from each participant's story.

Character Introduction and Team Formation:

The Three Little Pigs, known for their architectural skills, team up with Snow White, skilled in managing diverse personalities.

Their rival, the Big Bad Wolf, is introduced as having taken charisma lessons from Puss in Boots, aiming to diversify his skill set.

Competition Criteria Revealed: The judges, Fairy Godmother, the Cheshire Cat, and an unusually serious Humpty Dumpty, are introduced. They will judge the booths based on creativity, practicality, and a dash of magic, with an emphasis on incorporating story elements and regional crops.

Team Strategy and Construction:

The Three Little Pigs propose a brick booth that's wolf-proof.

Snow White suggests an apple-themed snack bar, emphasizing regional crops.

Dopey adds the idea of a mirror selfie station, while Grumpy insists on security measures against the Wolf.

Rival's Approach: The Big Bad Wolf focuses on a high-tech booth with holograms and flashy presentations, aiming for charm over substance.

The Competition:

Construction chaos with hammers, magic, and arguments over aesthetic choices among the pigs and Snow White's team.

The Wolf's booth initially impresses but ultimately reveals flaws, lacking in substance and proper representation of regional crops.

Judgment Day:

The Three Little Pigs and Snow White's booth, with its solid construction, apple motifs, and popular selfie station, stands out as a marvel of teamwork and enchantment.

The Wolf's booth's technological gimmicks fail, showing more style than substance.

Verdict and Aftermath:

The judges unanimously declare the Three Little Pigs, Snow White, and the dwarfs as winners.

The Wolf, in good spirits, proposes a joint venture for next year, suggesting a collaboration that could bring a new twist to their stories.

Resolution:

A hint at future collaboration is made with the exchange of handshakes and the possibility of a joint venture, leaving the story open for a sequel or continuation.

The story ends on a note of camaraderie, with even Grumpy making a kind gesture by handing the Wolf a basket of apples, leaving readers wondering about his true intentions.

Teacher Page

Plot Diagram

There is a PDF presentation for this as well as a Google Slide presentation at:
https://docs.google.com/presentation/d/1UdRNIrVVkpIwkdipBHQqVYffRtXhwv1veQSgWKwC7uU/edit?usp=sharing

The link is set to "Share with anyone who has the link" but this isn't always foolproof. Please check that it works, and you make a copy of the file before you need it. I respond to requests quickly, if there is an issue.

There are two versions of the plot diagram, both are represented in the presentations. Choose the version best suited to your students.

Exposition: This is where the setting and main characters are introduced. The story opens in a fantastical land where fairy tales and reality shows intersect, at a county fair renowned for its unique competition, the "Fairy Tale Mash-Up." Key characters include the Three Little Pigs, Snow White, the Big Bad Wolf, and the judges (Fairy Godmother, the Cheshire Cat, and Humpty Dumpty). The pigs and Snow White team up, while the Wolf decides to compete alone, hinting at his revamped charisma.

Conflict: The central conflict is introduced as a competition to design and construct the most enchanting and structurally sound booth at the fair, incorporating elements from their stories and regional crops. The underlying tension is the rivalry between the Three Little Pigs (and Snow White) and the Big Bad Wolf, fueled by their history and the Wolf's new charisma skills.

Rising Action: This phase includes several key developments:

> The Three Little Pigs propose a brick booth, Snow White suggests an apple-themed snack bar, and Dopey dreams up a mirror selfie station, while Grumpy focuses on security measures.
>
> The Big Bad Wolf, on the other hand, opts for a high-tech approach with holograms and flashy presentations, aiming to charm the audience.
>
> Both teams proceed with their construction, leading to a flurry of activity, including the use of magic, debates over aesthetics, and the implementation of high-tech gadgets by the Wolf.

Climax: The climax occurs on the day of the judging, where the efforts of both teams are put to the test. The booth of the Three Little Pigs and Snow White, with its sturdy construction, thematic decorations, and popular attractions, contrasts sharply with the Wolf's booth, which, while initially impressive, begins to show its technological gimmicks as more style than substance.

Falling Action: The judges deliver their unanimous verdict, declaring the Three Little Pigs, Snow White, and the dwarfs the winners of the competition. Their booth's combination of teamwork, durability, and enchantment outshines the Wolf's attempt at charm through technology.

Resolution: In the aftermath of the competition, the Wolf, rather than being discouraged, proposes a joint venture for the next year, suggesting a potential collaboration that could combine the best of both worlds. The story closes with the characters considering this proposition, signaling a new beginning and the promise of future adventures together.

This plot map outlines the narrative arc of your story, from the setup of the fairy tale county fair and introduction of the characters, through the building of tension and competition, to the climax of the competition's outcome, and finally resolving with the characters coming together in anticipation of future endeavors.

The County Fair
Plot Diagram

Exposition: This is where the setting and main characters are introduced. The story opens in a fantastical land where fairy tales and reality shows intersect, at a county fair renowned for its unique competition, the "Fairy Tale Mash-Up." Key characters include the Three Little Pigs, Snow White, the Big Bad Wolf, and the judges (Fairy Godmother, the Cheshire Cat, and Humpty Dumpty). The pigs and Snow White team up, while the Wolf decides to compete alone, hinting at his revamped charisma.

Conflict: The central conflict is introduced as a competition to design and construct the most enchanting and structurally sound booth at the fair, incorporating elements from their stories and regional crops. The underlying tension is the rivalry between the Three Little Pigs (and Snow White) and the Big Bad Wolf, fueled by their history and the Wolf's new charisma skills.

Rising Action: This phase includes several key developments:

The Three Little Pigs propose a brick booth, Snow White suggests an apple-themed snack bar, and Dopey dreams up a mirror selfie station, while Grumpy focuses on security measures.

The Big Bad Wolf, on the other hand, opts for a high-tech approach with holograms and flashy presentations, aiming to charm the audience.

Both teams proceed with their construction, leading to a flurry of activity, including the use of magic, debates over aesthetics, and the implementation of high-tech gadgets by the Wolf.

Climax: The climax occurs on the day of the judging, where the efforts of both teams are put to the test. The booth of the Three Little Pigs and Snow White, with its sturdy construction, thematic decorations, and popular attractions, contrasts sharply with the Wolf's booth, which, while initially impressive, begins to show its technological gimmicks as more style than substance.

Falling Action: The judges deliver their unanimous verdict, declaring the Three Little Pigs, Snow White, and the dwarfs the winners of the competition. Their booth's combination of teamwork, durability, and enchantment outshines the Wolf's attempt at charm through technology.

Resolution: In the aftermath of the competition, the Wolf, rather than being discouraged, proposes a joint venture for the next year, suggesting a potential collaboration that could combine the best of both worlds. The story closes with the characters considering this proposition, signaling a new beginning and the promise of future adventures together.

The County Fair
Plot Diagram

Exposition: This is where the setting and main characters are introduced. The story opens in a fantastical land where fairy tales and reality shows intersect, at a county fair renowned for its unique competition, the "Fairy Tale Mash-Up." Key characters include the Three Little Pigs, Snow White, the Big Bad Wolf, and the judges (Fairy Godmother, the Cheshire Cat, and Humpty Dumpty). The pigs and Snow White team up, while the Wolf decides to compete alone, hinting at his revamped charisma.

Conflict: The central conflict is introduced as a competition to design and construct the most enchanting and structurally sound booth at the fair, incorporating elements from their stories and regional crops. The underlying tension is the rivalry between the Three Little Pigs (and Snow White) and the Big Bad Wolf, fueled by their history and the Wolf's new charisma skills.

Rising Action: This phase includes several key developments:

The Three Little Pigs propose a brick booth, Snow White suggests an apple-themed snack bar, and Dopey dreams up a mirror selfie station, while Grumpy focuses on security measures.

The Big Bad Wolf, on the other hand, opts for a high-tech approach with holograms and flashy presentations, aiming to charm the audience.

Both teams proceed with their construction, leading to a flurry of activity, including the use of magic, debates over aesthetics, and the implementation of high-tech gadgets by the Wolf.

Climax: The climax occurs on the day of the judging, where the efforts of both teams are put to the test. The booth of the Three Little Pigs and Snow White, with its sturdy construction, thematic decorations, and popular attractions, contrasts sharply with the Wolf's booth, which, while initially impressive, begins to show its technological gimmicks as more style than substance.

Falling Action: The judges deliver their unanimous verdict, declaring the Three Little Pigs, Snow White, and the dwarfs the winners of the competition. Their booth's combination of teamwork, durability, and enchantment outshines the Wolf's attempt at charm through technology.

Resolution: In the aftermath of the competition, the Wolf, rather than being discouraged, proposes a joint venture for the next year, suggesting a potential collaboration that could combine the best of both worlds. The story closes with the characters considering this proposition, signaling a new beginning and the promise of future adventures together.

The County Fair
Plot Diagram

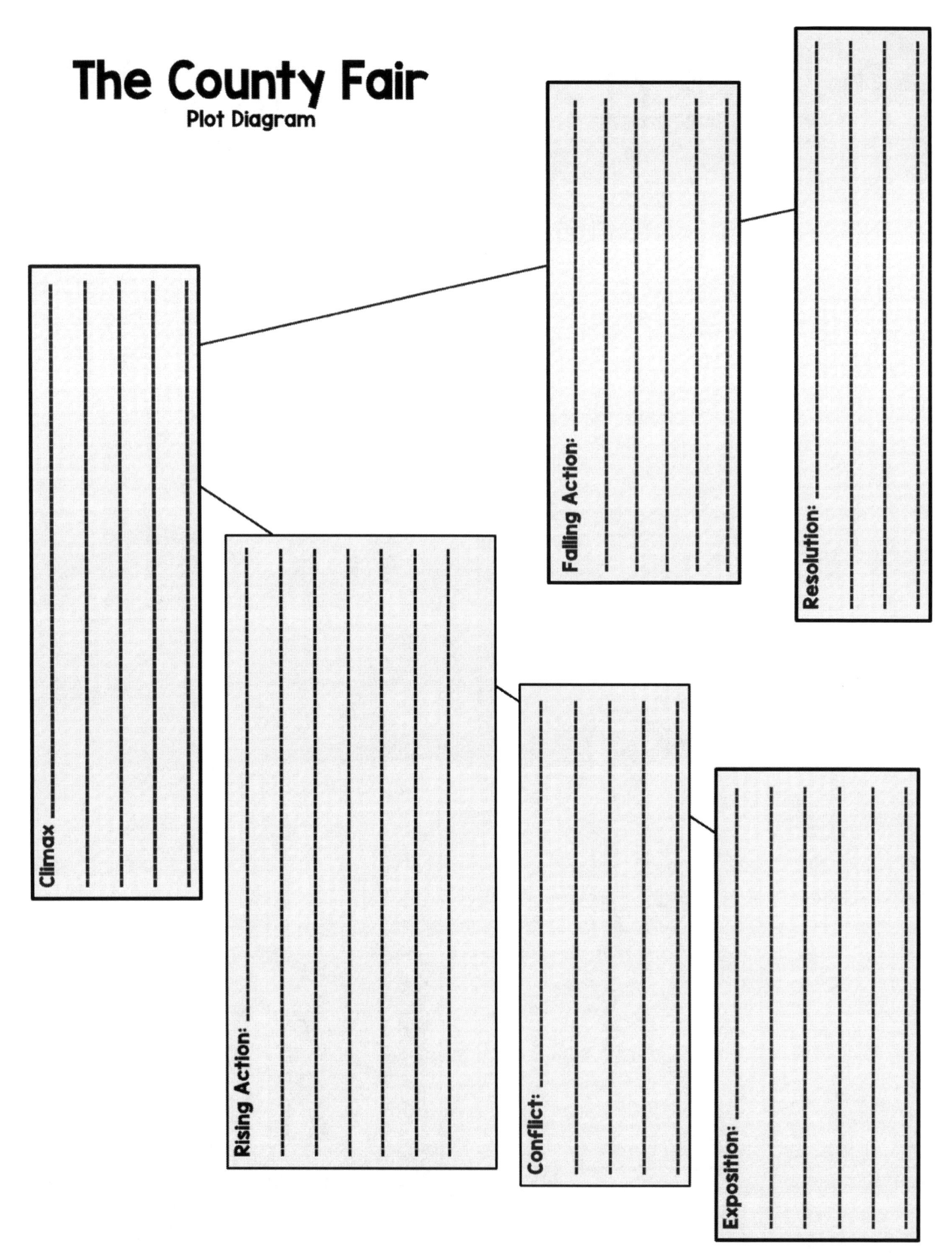

Climax

Rising Action:

Falling Action:

Resolution:

Conflict:

Exposition:

The County Fair 2
Plot Diagram

Climax: Judging day is here, and it's a big deal. The Pigs and Snow White's booth looks amazing and strong, full of cool things like apple decorations and a place to take selfies. The Wolf's booth looks cool at first with all its tech, but then it starts to fail and doesn't have much from where he lives, besides some mushrooms and straw.

Rising Action: The Pigs think of making a booth out of bricks, Snow White wants to add an apple snack bar, Dopey comes up with a selfie station idea, and Grumpy wants to make sure the Wolf doesn't cheat.

The Wolf decides to use high-tech tricks like holograms to win people over.

Both sides work hard on their booths, arguing about how things should look and trying out their ideas.

Conflict: Everyone is getting ready for a big contest at the fair. They need to build the coolest and strongest booth, using parts from their own stories and plants from where they live. The main problem is the competition between the Pig and Snow White team and the Wolf, who has been learning how to be more charming.

Falling Action: The judges decide that the Pigs, Snow White, and the dwarfs win because their booth is all about teamwork, it's strong, and it's truly magical. The Wolf's booth, even though it looked fancy, didn't really hold up.

Resolution: Even though the Wolf loses, he's not sad. He asks the Pigs and Snow White if they can work together next year, thinking they can come up with something even cooler together. The story ends with everyone thinking this might be a good idea, showing that they might team up for the next fair, and even Grumpy does something nice by giving the Wolf some apples.

Exposition: The story starts in a magical place where fairy tales and reality TV shows mix, at a very special county fair. We meet the main characters: the Three Little Pigs, Snow White, the Big Bad Wolf, and the judges (Fairy Godmother, the Cheshire Cat, and Humpty Dumpty). The Pigs and Snow White are one team, and the Wolf is on his own.

Name: _____   Partner: _____

The County Fair
Think - Pair - Share

Read "The County Fair"

Part 1: Think (Individual Work) – Answer the questions.

Characters: List the main characters and their traits. _____
_____
_____

Plot: Summarize the key events in the story. _____
_____
_____
_____

Themes: Identify the themes or moral lessons in the story. _____
_____
_____
_____

Part 2: Pair (Discussion with a Partner)
Questions for Discussion:
- What makes the characters unique?
- How do they solve the crisis?
- How does the setting contribute to the story?
- What are some real-life lessons that can be learned from this story?

Problem-Solving: Brainstorm ideas on how you could change or add to the story to make it more interesting.
_____
_____
_____
_____
_____
_____

Part 3: Be Prepared to Share Out

One new idea you heard during the discussion: _____
_____
_____
_____

One point you agreed/disagreed with and why: _____
_____
_____

Expand the Story - The County Fair Next Year

Task:
1. It's the next year. Write a narrative about what happens at the fair one year later. Use the characters from the original story, but feel free to add your own as well.
2. Practice and perform your fractured Fairy Tale.

Group Names: _____

Title: _____

Our Summary: _____

Name: _____ # _____

Expand the Story - The County Fair Next Year

Think of how you will fracture your tale. Write your ideas below.

Setting: _____

Twist or How Will Your Story be Fractured: _____

_____

_____

_____

Write the narrative of your story here:

Beginning: _____

_____

_____

_____

_____

_____

_____

_____

Middle: _____

_____

_____

_____

_____

_____

_____

End: _____

_____

_____

_____

_____

_____

_____

Name: _____ # _____

Elements of A Fairy Tale

Interactive notebook page.

	Original Fairy Tale	Our Version One Year Later
Who are the good characters?		
Who are the evil, bad or just misunderstood characters?		
What is the plot twist?		
Who is telling the story? (Point of View)		
What is the problem?		
What is the solution?		
What was the lesson learned?		

Glue under right column and attach to your paper. Fold along the dotted lines for an accordion fold.

Name: _____ # _____

Key Ideas and Detail RL.3 - Analyze the Author's Impact.
The County Fair

Analyze the Impact of the Author's Choices

Flap

AUTHOR CHOICES

- Setting
- Order of Action
- How the Characters are Introduced
- How the Characters are Developed
- Do You Like the Author's Choices? Use Evidence to Explain Why or Why Not
- What Would You Change?

Cut out the shape, cut along the dotted lines. Fold on the solid lines. Glue or tape under the flap.

Name: _____ # _____

Key Ideas and Detail RL.3 - Analyze the Author's Impact.
The County Fair

Analyze the Impact of the Author's Choices

1. **Setting:** The story takes place in a magical land where fairy tales and reality shows come together, specifically at a county fair known for its unique "Fairy Tale Mash-Up" competition. This setting is fun because it mixes the familiar elements of fairy tales with the excitement and drama of reality TV, creating a playful and imaginative backdrop for the events.

2. **Order of Action:** The story unfolds in a straightforward sequence. It begins with the introduction of the fair and the competition, followed by the team-up of the three little pigs and Snow White. They plan and build their booth, aiming to win against the Big Bad Wolf. The construction process, the presentation of their booth, and the judging phase lead up to the announcement of the winners. The story concludes with the possibility of future collaborations, especially between the traditional rivals. The clear sequence helps us understand how teamwork and creativity lead to success.

3. **How the Characters are Introduced:** Characters are introduced in an engaging way that quickly ties them to their fairy tale origins while also giving them a new twist. For example, the three little pigs are known architects, and Snow White is adept at managing diverse personalities. The Big Bad Wolf has been taking charisma lessons. This method of introduction is effective because it keeps the characters familiar to readers but also adds new layers to their personalities, making them fit perfectly in the story's unique setting.

4. **How the Characters are Developed:** The characters develop through their actions and interactions. For instance, Snow White's proposal of an apple-themed snack bar and the eldest pig's idea of a brick booth show their ability to merge traditional elements with new ideas. The Big Bad Wolf's attempt to charm with technology instead of substance reveals his character flaw. Through these developments, we see growth and adaptability in the characters, especially in their willingness to work together and value both old and new.

5. **Do You Like the Author's Choices?** Yes, the author's choices are quite likable because they create a story that's both entertaining and meaningful. By choosing a setting where fairy tales meet reality TV, the author brings a fresh twist to familiar characters, making the story interesting and dynamic. The mix of tradition and innovation in the booth's construction is a clever way to highlight the story's theme of collaboration and adaptability. Using well-known characters allows for immediate connection, while their development and the story's events offer new insights into teamwork and creativity.

6. **What Would You Change?** While the story is engaging as it is, adding a bit more detail about the competition itself and the other participants could make the world feel even richer. For example, mentioning a few other fairy tale characters and their projects could have added depth to the fair's competitive atmosphere and given readers a broader sense of the story's universe. Also, a bit more insight into the judges' thoughts during the competition could enhance the tension and excitement of the judging phase, making the victory even more rewarding.

Name: _____ # _____

Directions: Compare and contrast two different Fractured Fairy Tales from this Unit

_____vs. _____

What is the Main Idea of _____	What is the Main Idea of _____

3. List at least four things the two stories have in common. _____

_____

_____

_____

_____

4. List the main differences between the readings. _____

_____

_____

_____

_____

5. Which reading did you like best? _____

6. Explain why you like the reading you chose best. _____

_____

_____

_____

_____

The County Fair - Figurative Language

Name: _____ # _____

The County Fair - Figurative Language

In a realm where fables frolic with the frenzy of reality TV finales, there flourished a fair of unparalleled festivity. This fair, a fantastical fusion of fairy tale flair and television tumult, touted the "Fairy Tale Mash-Up" as its crowning jewel. A contest not for the faint-hearted, it was a battlefield where wit, will, and the wiles to withstand reality's roughest rumbles reigned supreme.

Among the myriad of magical participants, the three little pigs, animals of acceptable architecture, joined forces with Snow White, whose beauty was only eclipsed by her brilliance in balancing the boisterous bunch of dwarfs. Together, they were to lock horns with their legendary adversary, the Big Bad Wolf, now boasting a charm chiseled by the cunning craft of Puss in Boots. "Diversifying my skill set," he declared with a grin that glimmered with both guile and glamour.

Their Herculean task? To erect the most enchanting, structurally sound booth the county fair had ever seen, weaving wonders from their own worlds while showcasing the splendor of crops and relics of their regions. The panel of judges, a motley crew of magical magnificence, awaited creations crammed with creativity, practicality, and a pinch of the peculiar.

"I propose a fortress of bricks, as impervious to intrusion as the night is to light," proclaimed the eldest pig, his voice vibrating with valor. "And adorned with an apple-accented annex!" added Snow White, her optimism outshining the skepticism her suggestion spawned.

"But beware the bewitched," grumbled Grumpy, glaring at the gleeful gathering.

"We need a selfie station. Pictures and perfect apples!" mused Dopey, nearly toppling towers of technical texts.

Meanwhile, the Wolf wove a web of wonder, a booth brimming with the bravado of modernity, a mirage made real through the magic of machines. "Who needs the steadfastness of stone when you stand in the spectacle of simulations?" he boasted, his booth bathing bystanders in a ballet of beams.

As judgment day dawned, the fairground was aflutter with anticipation. The collaborative creation of the pigs and Snow White stood steadfast, its brick bones bearing the burden of beauty and brawn, its apple-themed offerings an ode to origins, drawing droves of delighted fair-goers.

Name: _____ # _____

The County Fair - Figurative Language - page 2

In contrast, the Wolf's wondrous world wavered, its holographic heroes flickering into fables, revealing a reliance on razzle over real.

The verdict was voiced with unanimous vigor. Victory was vested in the valorous venture of the pigs and Snow White, a testament to the triumph of teamwork, tradition, and a touch of the times. "Substance over style," snickered Doc, as accolades were awarded.

Yet, in a twist of fate, the Wolf, wistful but wise, whispered of a wish to weave their talents together come next conclave. "Perhaps there's merit in melding minds," mused the eldest pig, proffering a paw in peace. And so, amid amiable adieus and apples offered in amends, a new narrative was nurtured, hinting at the harmony of hearts once at hedge.

Name: _____ # _____

The County Fair - Figurative Language

Directions: Tell what type of figurative language the sample from the reading is and what it means.

Example: Alliteration: "fables frolic with the frenzy of reality TV finales"
   Type: Alliteration
   Explanation: This uses the repetition of the initial 'f' sound to create a rhythmic and evocative description of the fair's environment, making the scene lively and vibrant.

1. "a battlefield where wit, will, and the wiles to withstand reality's roughest rumbles reigned supreme."

   Type: _____

   Explanation: _____
   _____

2. "as impervious to intrusion as the night is to light,"

   Type: _____

   Explanation: _____
   _____

3. "a grin that glimmered with both guile and glamour."

   Type: _____

   Explanation: _____
   _____

4. "a booth brimming with the bravado of modernity, a mirage made real through the magic of machines."

   Type: _____

   Explanation: _____
   _____

5. "The verdict was voiced with unanimous vigor. The verdict was the victory was vested in the valorous venture"

   Type: _____

   Explanation: _____
   _____

6. "amid amiable adieus and apples offered in amends,"

   Type: _____

   Explanation: _____
   _____

Name: _____ # _____

The County Fair - Figurative Language

Presentation for this worksheet:
https://docs.google.com/presentation/d/1QeDP34Bzplc0oRvkw2zcLaDkD9gYLBRb46K3I_EahXU/edit?usp=sharing

Directions: Tell what type of figurative language the sample from the reading is and what it means.

Example: Alliteration: "fables frolic with the frenzy of reality TV finales"
  Type: Alliteration
  Explanation: This uses the repetition of the initial 'f' sound to create a rhythmic and evocative description of the fair's environment, making the scene lively and vibrant.

1. **Metaphor:** "a battlefield where wit, will, and the wiles to withstand reality's roughest rumbles reigned supreme."
  Type: Metaphor
  Explanation: This phrase compares the competition to a battlefield without using "like" or "as," suggesting that the contest is intense and requires strategy and strength, much like a real battle.

2. **Simile:** "as impervious to intrusion as the night is to light,"
  Type: Simile
  Explanation: Here, the steadfastness of the proposed brick fortress is compared to the night's ability to block out light, using "as" to highlight the complete protection it offers.

3. **Personification:** "a grin that glimmered with both guile and glamour."
  Type: Personification
  Explanation: This gives human qualities (glimmering with guile and glamour) to the Wolf's grin, enhancing his cunning and charming nature in a vivid way.

4. **Hyperbole:** "a booth brimming with the bravado of modernity, a mirage made real through the magic of machines."
  Type: Hyperbole
  Explanation: This exaggeration emphasizes the Wolf's booth's high-tech allure, suggesting it's so advanced and impressive that it seems like a magical mirage come to life.

5. **Repetition:** "The verdict was voiced with unanimous vigor. The verdict was the victory was vested in the valorous venture"
  Type: Repetition
  Explanation: The repetition of the words "the verdict" adds emphasis

6. **Alliteration:** "amid amiable adieus and apples offered in amends,"
  Type: Alliteration
  Explanation: The repetition of the 'a' sound here creates a soothing and harmonious ending, emphasizing the peace and goodwill achieved among the characters.

7. **Metaphor:** "wove a web of wonder,"
  Type: Metaphor
  Explanation: This metaphor suggests the Wolf's booth is so enthralling and complex that it's like a web, capturing the attention of all who see it, without using "like" or "as" for comparison.

Name: _____ # _____

Compare and Contrast - Story vs. Readers Theater

Directions: Please use complete sentences to answer the questions.

Version Title: _____

How are the characters in the reader's theater script similar to the characters in the story?
_____
_____
_____

How are the settings and dialogue in the reader's theater script different from those in the story?
_____
_____
_____

How are the settings and dialogue in the reader's theater script the same as those in the story?
_____
_____
_____

How does the use of dialogue in the reader's theater script enhance the story differently than the narrative form?
_____
_____
_____
_____

What are the main events in both the reader's theater script and the narrative, and how are they presented differently in each version?	
Reader's Theater Script Main Events	Narrative or Story Main Events
Similarities:	Similarities:
Differences:	Differences:

Research Based Fluency Practice

Why Fluency?

To be considered "on level" in reading fluency, students should be able to read aloud an unrehearsed passage, (i.e., either narrative or expository, fiction or non-fiction that is 200 to 300 words in length) from a grade-level text, with at least 95% accuracy in word reading. As students read aloud, their reading should sound as effortless as if they were speaking (Hasbrouck & Glaser, 2012.) This does not come easily for some students, which is why fluency practice is so essential.

In order to be considered fluent readers, students in grades 9 through 12 should be able to correctly read 150 words per minute (Hasbrouck & Tindal, 2006). In 2006 and again in 2010, Hasbrouck and Hasbrouck and Tindal (respectively) put forth that "[i]t is sufficient for students to read unpracticed, grade-level text at the 50th percentile of oral reading fluency norms" and that "...teachers do not need to have students read faster because there is no evidence that reading faster than the 50th percentile increases comprehension." See chart below.

The best strategy for developing and improving reading fluency is to provide students with many opportunities to read the same passages orally several times. These exercises provide such opportunities. On each passage, there is space for reading fluency calculations. The best part is that the passages are quick and make it easy for students to read aloud repeatedly – and often – without taking up a lot of valuable classroom time. The activities can also be spread over several days.

In an updated 2017 study, Hasbrouck & Tindal reported that "students scoring 10 or more words below the 50th percentile using the average score of two unpracticed readings from grade-level materials need a fluency-building program. Teachers can also use the table to set long-term fluency goals for struggling readers."

Research suggests that one of the easiest and most effective ways for high school teachers to address reading fluency is to implement quick timed fluency into their weekly schedules.

Grade	Percentile	Fall WPM	Winter WPM	Spring WPM	Grade	Percentile	Fall WPM	Winter WPM	Spring WPM
1	90		81	111	5	90	166	182	194
1	75		47	82	5	75	139	156	168
1	50		23	53	5	50	110	127	139
1	25		12	28	5	25	85	99	109
1	10		6	15	5	10	61	74	83
2	90	106	125	142	6	90	177	195	204
2	75	79	100	117	6	75	153	167	177
2	50	51	72	89	6	50	127	140	150
2	25	25	42	61	6	25	98	111	122
2	10	11	18	31	6	10	68	82	93
3	90	128	146	162	7	90	180	192	202
3	75	99	120	137	7	75	156	165	177
3	50	71	92	107	7	50	128	136	150
3	25	44	62	78	7	25	102	109	123
3	10	21	36	48	7	10	79	88	98
4	90	145	166	180	8-12	90	185	199	199
4	75	119	139	152	8-12	75	161	173	177
4	50	94	112	123	8-12	50	133	146	151
4	25	68	87	98	8-12	25	106	115	125
4	10	45	61	72	8-12	10	77	84	97

Lexile Measures

Lexile measures can play an important role in supporting and developing fluency. Here's how:

1. **Gradual Increase in Complexity:** By knowing a student's Lexile measure, educators can select texts that are just right in terms of difficulty. Starting with texts at or slightly below a student's Lexile measure allows the student to practice fluency without being overly burdened by challenging vocabulary or complex sentence structures. As fluency improves, the complexity of the texts can gradually increase.

2. **Repeated Reading:** One of the proven strategies for improving fluency is repeated reading, where a student reads the same text multiple times. Using Lexile measures, you can select texts that are a good fit for this purpose, ensuring that the text is challenging enough to be beneficial but not so difficult that it frustrates the reader.

3. **Targeted Intervention:** For students struggling with fluency, Lexile measures can help you pinpoint specific areas of need. For instance, if a student has a high comprehension level but reads very slowly, it's clear that fluency is the primary challenge.

4. **Progress Monitoring:** As students practice fluency, they'll often progress to texts with higher Lexile levels. By regularly assessing students' reading with texts of increasing Lexile measures, educators can monitor growth in fluency over time.

5. **Building Confidence:** Reading fluency is also tied to confidence. By providing students with texts at their Lexile level, they experience success, which can boost their confidence. As their confidence grows, so does their willingness to take on more challenging texts, further enhancing their fluency.

6. **Parental Involvement:** Educators can communicate Lexile measures to parents, giving them a clearer understanding of their child's reading level. Parents can then provide reading materials at home that match their child's Lexile range, offering additional opportunities for fluency practice.

Lexile Grade Level Reading Chart

Grade	Far Below	Approaching Grade Level	Meets Grade Level	Exceeds Grade Level
1	111 L and Below	110L – 185L	190L-530L	535L and Above
2	150L and Below	115L-415L	420L-650L	655L and Above
3	265L and Below	270L-515L	520L-820L	825L and Above
4	385L and Below	390L-735L	740L-940L	945L and Above
5	500L and Below	505L-825L	830L-1010L	1015L and Above
6	555L and Below	560L-920L	925-1070L	1075L and Above
7	625L and Below	630L-965L	970L-1120L	1125L and Above
8	660L and Below	665L – 1005L	1010L – 1185L	1190L and Above
9	775L and Below	780L-1045L	1050L-1260L	1265L and Above
10	830L and Below	835L-1075L	1080L – 1335L	1340 and Above
11 & 12	950 L and Below	995L-1180L	1185-1385L	1390L and Above

This is an evidence-based program, and it works.

Begin each passage as a guided reading. This is an evidence-based strategy for improving reading fluency. The student is asked to read the same passage three to five times, receiving feedback each time from the instructor or peer reviewer. Since this program is peer-to-peer, feedback comes from peers. By providing feedback on accuracy, rate and expression, students can incorporate those changes into each subsequent reading, eventually reaching a point of fluency with that particular passage. They can then move on to more difficult assignments.

Repeated readings of text can also contribute to better comprehension, one of the cornerstones of reading throughout life. All schools, from elementary to college, can easily provide students with repeated readings as well as paired passages of the same theme or topic.

For those teachers who want to mix-up full-class fluency lessons, one option is fluency-oriented reading instruction (FORI). This evidence-based practice begins with a teacher reading a particular passage aloud while students follow along in silent reading. Then, students read the passage aloud numerous times throughout the week, including echo, choral and partner reading. They also practice the passage for 15-30 minutes daily. At the end of a week, students engage in discussion, writing an essay or performing other activities that prove comprehension of the passage.

Why Lexile Measures and Fluency?

Lexiles help us measure the levels at which one reads fluently. Lexiles range from 200 for beginning readers to 1700 for advanced readers. Lexile text below 200 represents beginning-reading material, and a student's Lexile score may have a number in the 100s or the code of BR. BR is a code that stands for Beginning Reading. When reading at a students appropriate Lexile level, comprehension should be at least 75%.

What are the reading demands of the post-secondary world according to Lexile Measures?

Median Text Measures (Williamson, 2004):
11th/12th grade (LA/SS textbooks):	(1090L)
GED Test Materials:	(1060L)
SAT/ACT Test Materials:	(1180L)
Military (training/field manuals):	(1180L)
Citizenship (newspapers, voting, jury):	(1230L)
Workplace (Daggett study materials):	(1260L)
Postsecondary - first two yrs. (textbooks):	(1355L)
University	(1395L)
Community College	(1295L)

Why do high schoolers need to practice fluency? An examination of K-12 texts using Lexile levels reveals a gap of 65L to 230L between high school seniors and the difficulty of postsecondary texts. Texts required for postsecondary college and career fall within a Lexile range of 1200L to 1400L, while the text complexity of typical high school textbooks for grades 11 and 12 is about 1050L to 1165L. This research provides valuable insight into the apparent disconnect when high school graduates encounter college and career texts. To put this gap in perspective, a 250L difference between reader ability and text complexity can cause a drop from 75-percent comprehension to 50-percent comprehension. This means that high school seniors who can successfully read twelfth-grade texts may enter college or the workplace several months later and encounter texts that result in less than 50-percent comprehension (Williamson, 2008).

Please see research references on the last page of this manual.

**These passages are designed to check and
increase fluency at the high school level.**

This programs works for resource, whole class, RTI, and summer school. If you are using this program with more than one students – partner up. Partnering students is engaging and lets everyone participate. I find that students helping students builds confidence and reinforces learning; additionally, by reading, tracking and reading again, student exposure to each passage is maximized. Research suggests that pairing readings with like-level reading partners is motivating and increases reading success.

INSTRUCTIONS AND SCRIPT

Before you begin, have a copy of one passage for each student. The PDF can be displayed before the whole class on a Smartboard or printed and projected on a document camera. As you explain the lessons, demonstrate what students will be doing.

Explain what fluency is - the rate and ease at which we read along with the flow of reading.

About breaking students into pairs. If you are working with a group of students with varying abilities - pair like-leveled students together.

Explain the entire activity, as well as how to calculate combined words per minute, or CWPM. Then read the passage aloud. Have students track on their sheets as you read aloud. It is extremely beneficial for struggling students to hear the passage before they read it aloud. The goal isn't to have students stumble, but to optimize opportunities for ultimate success.

The first few times you do fluency as a class – the script below may be helpful:

1. **Check to make sure each person is in the right spot and then read the passage.**
2. **After you read the selected passage aloud, partner students and say something like:** *Put your name on your paper. Since you need to be marking your partner's paper, switch papers now. Raise your hand if you are Partner 1.*
3. **Pause until one student from each pair has their hand raised – acknowledge students when one person of each pair has their hand raised.**
4. **Raise your hand if you are Partner 2.** Pause until the other student from each pair has their hand raised – acknowledge students when the other partner has their hand raised.

    Excellent. When I say "Begin", all Partner 1s should quietly begin to read to their partners.

    All Partner 2s will use their pencils to keep track of their partner's errors. Partner 2s will put a line over each word pronounced incorrectly.

    When the timer goes off, all Partner 2s will circle the last word read, but Partner 1s will keep reading until the passage is complete. Does anyone have any questions?

5. **Set the timer for one minute. If there are no questions -** *Begin.*
6. **When the timer goes off give chance for students to finish:** *Partner 2s, please mark your partner's score and give feedback to Partner 1s. To calculate CWPM subtract the number of errors from the total number of words read.*
7. **Walk around the room to make sure scores are being marked correctly.**
8. **Make sure students are ready and then switch for Partner 2s to read.**

    Ready? Begin.

Made in the USA
Middletown, DE
08 October 2024